Through the Darkest Valley

Through the Darkest Valley

*The Lament Psalms and One Woman's Lifelong Battle
Against Depression*

Teresa S. Smith

RESOURCE *Publications* · Eugene, Oregon

THROUGH THE DARKEST VALLEY
The Lament Psalms and One Woman's Lifelong Battle Against Depression

Resource Publishing
A Division of Wipf and Stock Publishers
199 W. 8th Ave., Suite 3
Eugene, OR 97401
www.wipfandstock.com

ISBN 13: 978-1-60608-528-8

Manufactured in the U.S.A.

For those whose stories bind them,
whose wounds cry out in the night,
and those who battle the monsters with them.

Contents

Foreword ix

Prologue: Slaying the Monster xi

1 The Great Escape 1
     Domestic Violence Information

2 The Dragon's History 10
     The Origins of Domestic Violence

3 Free Fall 16
     Sexual Abuse Information

4 A Baby Step Toward Healing 28
     Healthy Relationships

5 Leaps of Faith 37
     Counseling Information

6 Intersections and Decisions 46
     How I Began to Heal

7 The Way of the World 60
     Racism, Sexism, and Justice Information

8 Four Churches and a Mountain 73
     Behavior Modification and Forgiveness Information

9   Matchmaker, Matchmaker 86
        Finding the Right Help for You

10 A Year of Hope 93
        Hope Information

11 Transitions Galore! 103
        Prayer Changes Things

12 The Journey of Suffering 119
        Depression Prevention Information

13 Sunshine, Sea Changes, and Surprises 133
        Dysthymia and Self-esteem Information

14 Suffering Reborn 147
        Anger Information

15 The Unstoppable Setting Sun 161
        Anxiety and Stress Information

16 Stumbling in the Dark 173
        Medication Information

17 Midnight and a Million Prayers 184
        Lament Psalms Information

18 Climbing Out of the Pit 193
        All Things Work Together

Foreword

THIS IS MY STORY, seen through *my* eyes. My story is filtered through my experiences, abilities, weaknesses, and particular make up. Were you to ask my mother and father, they would tell you that I am different from my siblings. These differences give me a viewpoint on people, places, and experiences that is mine alone. A good example is that of my great-grandparents. One of my cousins remembers large jars filled with candy in their garage. I don't remember candy; I remember eating delicious frozen pies each time we were at their house.

At the end of each chapter, I have placed practical concrete information designed to give you information and encouragement if you are facing a dark valley such as depression, domestic violence, sexual abuse, or the like. However, I am not a psychiatrist or a counselor; I am a United Methodist minister. I have included Scriptures to increase your faith. Discussion questions can be found at the end of each chapter. I have changed many names and descriptions in order that my family and others may have a modicum of privacy.

This book is designed to show you the way I have found healing and hope. It is not intended to give you the definitive answers regarding what medications you may need or which exercises will aid in your healing. Everyone's journey is different. May the blessings of God be upon you and your journey!

Prologue

Slaying the Monster

GARY NELSON, IN HIS book *Relentless Hope*, calls depression a monster. Nelson says it is not the person choosing to "act" a certain way; it's the depression/monster acting out. Depression is not a feeling that comes and goes throughout the day. At its root, depression is the experience of unshakable emptiness, hopelessness, or helplessness that lasts more than two weeks. (More information can be found online at www.healthprofessor .com. Click "Emotional Care.") Possible signs include:

- No pleasure in life, even in activities one used to enjoy
- Life is difficult and hard. Every decision is enormous.
- Thoughts of worthlessness, death, and hopelessness
- Phrases like: "What's the point?" "Damned if I do; damned if I don't." "Who cares?" become the answer to eating, hygiene, and fun.
- Tired all the time or have great difficulty sleeping
- Lack of energy, a huge sense of guilt, or inability to make everyday decisions
- Repetitive thoughts about death or suicide
- Work all the time
- In tears throughout the day
- Use food, drugs, or alcohol to "treat" the depression
- Uncontrollable rage, out of nowhere

Depression is not a choice or an act; it is an illness. When I am in the depths of depression, I am unable to do battle with it. The first step in slaying the monster is to receive treatment: counseling and medication. With these reinforcements I become armed for battle and I am able to join the battle against it.

This is the way I battle monsters like depression, while receiving counseling and medication. I *slay* the monster. See. Learn. Act. Yes!

See. I become aware of an unhealthy pattern or symptom.

Learn. I work hard to learn everything I can about the cause and possible solutions.

Act. I choose a new way and begin to practice it, with the support of my family and friends.

Yes! Every time I succeed in doing it the new way, I affirm myself out loud.

1

The Great Escape

The afternoon sunshine pierced us and lit up the chaff on our necks and arms. Standing on the wagon, putting another hay bale onto the elevator, I glimpsed Dad coming around the corner.

"Here he comes with rain on the brain," I said to my younger sister, Lisa, who was on the wagon with me.

"What are you doing?" Dad bellowed. "It's going to rain! Get a move on. Lisa, go up and help mow." Dad leapt up on the wagon and began slinging bales like lightning.

When the wagon was empty, he started up the old John Deere and hauled me with the wagon out to the hayfield.

"What are you doing?" he bellowed at Mom, who was stacking bales on the wagon. "Let's go," he ordered my little brother. Brother didn't move fast enough. Dad shoved him aside, pulled out the throttle.

He cussed. "What were you thinking? Rain's on the way." He continued to berate my brother. If Dad kept it up, I knew he'd hit my brother.

"Stop it!" I shouted. "It's not his fault. Stop treating him like that." Dad swung around on the tractor and in the blink of an eye he was on the wagon with me.

"What did you say?" he asked, breathing fire.

"I said, stop treating him that way or I'm going home," I said defiantly.

"Go home then. Just *go*." Sweat ran down his red face, his eyes blazed. "I said, *go home!*"

Jumping off the wagon, I headed home. Too angry to realize I didn't have to help with the hay anymore, I sobbed the whole two-mile walk home. I was oblivious to the fact I was leaving for college in the morning.

∾∾∾

"I am not coming back," my feet said as they carried a box out of the house and down the worn back steps. The screen door banged shut behind me. After loading the last few things into the old mustard-yellow Opal, I wired the broken trunk shut. There, under the sun-dappled shade of the giant maple trees lining the driveway, the flies buzzed lazily.

My brothers and sister had already gotten on the school bus as if it were an ordinary day. Dad had driven off at seven o'clock to roof a hip barn. After feeding the steers, Mom took the quarter-ton truck and headed out to take more shingles to Dad. The smell of newly cut hay mixed with the ever-present odor of manure. I made one final run through the house.

I grabbed a cookie, did one last sweep of my room, and I was off! I shot out of the driveway and within minutes I was leaning in on the highway's yellow double-striped line.

Never again. No more. No more tyrant ruling my life. No more fights would hold me captive 'til my gut ached. Done. Eighteen, and on my own.

Heading out, I sang with the radio for the sheer joy of it. The University of Wisconsin-Stout was hours away. My mind reviewed the situation. All of my life I had felt inferior, less important than the town kids with their trendy clothes and fun-focused lives. In spite of doing demonstration contests in 4-H and giving speeches, I had been tongue-tied in public. It was like I had a split personality. At home I was brash, mouthy, and quick to anger, pretending to eat fear for breakfast while dishing out sarcasm at supper. According to my dad, "The older you get, the dumber you are." I was unable to finish a task to meet his satisfaction. According to my mom I was helpful and smart.

At the hospital pharmacy where I had worked, I was steadily given raises and more responsibility, but I waited in fear for my boss and co workers to figure out who I really was. In high school I took the vocational level courses, telling myself I wanted to stay away from the snobs, who, I believed, were cheaters. I was on the outskirts of cliques, friendly with most everyone, close to almost no one.

∾∾∾

On the interstate the truck drivers saw my young, freckled face and long, brown hair flying. They honked and waved. I grinned and whizzed up and down the rolling hills. Here, Brown Swiss cows, and there, Holstein cows filled the pastures. I vowed my life would be better. I was going to start over. No more shy girl. No more taking easy classes and avoiding people. No more taking abuse. No more.

August of 1981. This was my new life. Rolling into Menominee, Wisconsin, was glorious. I had arrived! Winding my way through the small-town streets, I worried about finding my dorm.

Finally pulling up, I stared at what appeared to be a festival: a riot of families and loads of stuff. U-Hauls were parked every which way. Dads were carrying lumber up the stairs. Moms were waiting by the elevator with siblings and stacks of boxes, trunks, and laundry baskets. I raced up the three flights like a rabbit pursued by a hawk. No trudging for me.

Room 301. This was it. I took a deep breath and entered.

Breezing into the room, I announced, "Hi, I'm Teresa."

My neon smile dimmed as a quiet girl turned around. She spoke with a lisp, "I'm Ginnie. This is my mother, Jackie Breyes."

My independent heart sank. I looked over Ginnie's five-foot frame, and her perfectly matched shirt and shorts from my height of five feet, five inches. Then I contemplated my own cut-off shorts and faded tee shirt proclaiming, "I'm proud to be a Farmer's Daughter!"

After I had carried the rest of my stuff up the three flights to my room, Jackie asked, "Where are you from?" I gave her a short answer; I was more intent on pulling my cornflower blue blanket out of a box. I began to make the bed.

Ginnie and her mom surveyed the small closet and dresser and compared it to the pile of belongings they had brought into our small room.

"Honey, I'll just have to take your winter things home and leave your fall things here. When you need them, I'll bring them back," Ginnie's mom said, then she turned to me. Her carefully painted toenails and dainty sandals were everything my mother was not.

"Teresa, would you like to go to the dining hall with us?" she asked, her short, prim haircut perfect in every way.

"Oh," I searched for a polite reply. "No, I ate on the way here. Thanks for asking." Even with my belongings stowed in the closet, you could have set off an echo in there. The dresser had as much air space as clothing in it. I ventured down the hallway. Adrenaline carried me to each doorway. I leaned in. "Hey, I'm Teresa!"

The woman across the hall looked up and said, "I'm Donna from Iron Eagle. I just transferred in." She was quiet and tall.

Her roommate spun around, lit up, and said, "I'm Janice from Dane County." She said it with a flourish and a bow. Immediately, I was hooked on her dramatic approach to life. She was lithe and confident. Working my way down the hall, almost skipping, I stuck my head in door after door. Bev. Sue. Teresa. Debbie. Mary. Cheryl. Roxanne. Jenny. Jill. Anne. Erin. Rita. I memorized their faces and knew I owned this place. Back in Janice's room, I flopped on her bed.

Janice spoke with flair, "I lived in Svveeeeden for a year. So . . . you are a farmer's daughter. Where's the farm?" Her limp, dark-blonde hair swung about her chin, framing her face. Janice's hips swiveled and shimmied, like a belly dancer—she managed to make putting away clothes look like an exotic movie.

Janice and I went to register for classes. In the huge, crowded gym, I took out my checkbook and paid the tuition from my own account. At $1,500 for room, board, and tuition, it was the largest check I had ever written.

English 101, Geography, and Introduction to Vocational Rehabilitation all rolled along without a hitch. I had been yearning to learn more about the Bible. My friend, Donna, shared my desire. We started taking walks together and talked about our beliefs. Her serious eyes took me in and held me tenderly. Together, we agreed to pray about things.

Rita and I had some of the same classes. It was hard to believe we were friends. She had been a cheerleader in high school! We were both majoring in Vocational Rehabilitation. It was odd. Here I thought I was average, but she was working really hard to get good grades and I was sailing.

One day, when Rita and I were hanging out, I gave her a friendly punch in the arm. Suddenly, she was holding her arm as if she were thwarting a major flow of blood from a fresh wound.

"Teresa! Owwwww! That hurt."

I was puzzled. No one in my family would have ever admitted a punch in the arm hurt. Silently, I vowed never to punch another friend.

☙ ☙ ☙

Late September. Early morning. Someone knocked hard on my door.

"Phone call for you, Teresa!"

Sleepy and surprised, I hurried down the long tiled hallway. Who would it be at this hour? Long distance calls were reserved for emergencies in my family.

"Hello?"

At the sound of my dad's voice, I sunk to the floor. As far as I knew, my dad had never dialed a phone, not even once in his life. We kids or Mom had always done it for him.

"Teres," he said, shakily, "Ma's in the hospital and she may not live. Don't come now; there's nothing you can do. She's in Intensive Care, and has a 50–50 chance of making it. She inhaled silage gas on Sunday night." He was crying as he talked. My dad never cried.

"Do you need a bus ticket to come home this weekend?" he asked.

Now I was really confused; didn't he remember I drove to college? In a daze, I walked back to my room and fell back on my rumpled bed. There I prayed, and prayed, and prayed. I prayed for God's will to be done. I prayed for Jesus to show me the way.

A sense of peace came over me; it was a peace that didn't make any sense. I heard a voice, full of assurance. It would be all right if Mom lived. It would be all right if Mom died. God would take care of it. I could trust God. Unbeknownst to me, prayer chains had been activated all over my hometown. Hundreds of Christians were praying for my mom.

Wait until Friday to go home? Dad must be crazy. Why would I stay away? What had really happened? Why did he wait until Tuesday to call me? The accident happened on Sunday!

I responded on autopilot, following his directions. He was the tyrant, and I was the unwilling follower, once again the helpless child. As soon as classes finished on Friday, I ran to the distant parking lot. The five-hour drive took forever.

Arriving at the hospital, I parked and made a beeline up the hill. Déjà vu. This was where I had worked in the pharmacy for two years, up until just a month ago.

A rubber-soled hush filled the antiseptic hallway. I passed by knots of grieving, shocked people in the waiting-room doorway. Stopping at the Intensive Care Unit's double doors, I breathlessly rang the bell.

The person answered in a starched voice, "May I help you?"

"I'm here to see LeeAnn." My hands were trembling; my voice sounded foreign to me.

"Are you family?" she asked.

"Yes, I am her daughter."

"Come in. She's in room three."

Entering the ICU wasn't business as usual, like when I had delivered medicine for the pharmacy. I talked to myself, *Remember she's on a respirator, with intravenous tubes and a catheter. You've seen it before, Teresa. It's okay.*

Crossing the curtained threshold of room three, I took a sharp breath. It felt like someone had punched me.

"Hi, Mom," I called out softly, in a chipper voice. Her pale blue eyes opened. Although her eyes followed me, she didn't move. I leaned over the bed rail and held her calloused hand while I tried to think of what to say.

"Dad called me. School's been going fine. It must've been a long week." I fell silent, shifted my weight. "Rita and I've been going for walks after supper. I guess we go about two miles. Donna, my neighbor across the hall, has been praying for you."

There was soft laughter at the nurses' station. Mom's respirator rhythmically moved her chest up and down. I stared at the wall.

"Mom, do you want me to pray with you?" I asked. Her head nodded ever so slightly. "Our Father, who art in heaven, hallowed be thy name. Thy kingdom come; thy will be done . . ." I was grasping for words—it was like trying to catch a bird that was loose in my brain, ". . . on earth as it is in heaven. Give us this day our daily bread. Forgive us our trespasses, as we forgive those who trespass against us." Tears were threatening, I pressed hard through the last words. "Lead us not into temptation. Deliver us from evil. For thine is the kingdom, the power, and the glory forever. Amen."

I squeezed her hand and said in a choked-up voice, "I'll see you tomorrow. I love you." Tears broke loose before I could get out of the room.

Driving through town and back into the countryside, I was once again on autopilot. It was as if Johnnie's Diner, the corner gas station, and the Piggly Wiggly didn't exist. In the driveway I parked near the cellar door.

Home was just as I had left it. As the back door banged shut behind me, I heard my married sister, Andrea, in the kitchen. Her quick footsteps moved from stove to sink to the old oak table my mom had refinished.

"Hi, Andi," I said. "I didn't know you would be here."

"Well, you know . . ." her voice trailed off.

"So what's the week been like? Where's Dad?"

She paused for a moment, then answered, "He's down cellar. He's so upset, all he does is cry. Mom's had a really rough week. The silage gas turned into nitric acid in her lungs. They say most people die from it, don't live through the first night. But they have a new respirator called PEEP:

Positive End Respiration. Each time it 'breathes,' it forces a little more air into the lungs to keep them from collapsing, and to stop the acid from eating them up. The outlook isn't so grim now. But, she's not out of the woods yet."

I tried to absorb the information. "Where are your kids?"

"They're with Grandma."

The flat chocolate-chip cookie crumbled, as I bit into it. Then I remembered a bit of news about our other sister. "Oh, Barb's coming home; but I don't know when."

"I need to go home soon; it's almost milking time," Andi said.

"Okay."

We hugged, and she called down the steps to tell Dad she was leaving. I tried to bury my sadness. Then I went down the steps, saucepan in hand. Walking back toward the root cellar to get potatoes, I ran straight into Dad.

He was sitting on an upside-down five-gallon pail. The bare light bulb made a circle of light above him. It dimly lit the shelves full of canned fruit and vegetables. Dad looked oddly old; though he was only forty-something.

"Hi." I stood near him awkwardly.

He looked up and with a creaking voice said, "Hey, Teres', have you been to the hospital?"

"Yah, I stopped on my way here." I immediately reverted to the Swiss form of "yes."

"How is she?" He glanced up at me with watery eyes, then looked down again.

"She looks like somebody in Intensive Care. She seemed to know I was there; but she didn't really have any strength." I leaned back against the chest freezer and inhaled the slightly smoky air.

He began to tell the story. "She went up the silo chute, at the other farm, with the heavy-duty electrical cord tied around her waist. She was getting ready to hook up the silo unloader. You know, level out the mounded silage and lower the unloader so it would work in the morning. The loader tractor was revved way up to keep the blower running and the poisonous gas out. Next thing I knew the cord wasn't moving; she wasn't moving up the chute. I tried to go up after her, but the fumes were too bad. I had to go up the outside ladder to get her out and help her down.

"She rested under the tree, seemed to be all right. Later, we figured out the blower sheared a pin, so the tractor kept going at full throttle but no air was blowing through the pipes. She played with the grandkids that night. After midnight, she started coughing up blood. It was awful! They still don't know if she's going to live," he said with tears streaming down his face.

He went back to puttering. I retrieved the potatoes and put them into the saucepan. There was nothing more to say. Dad didn't answer questions; he only asked them.

∾∾∾

On Sunday, as I headed back to college, I felt disconnected. It had been a shock to see my dad broken and crying. What happened to the bellowing, red-faced maniac who ate and breathed work? Where did Dad, the dictator, go? What happened to the fire-breathing dragon that lived within him? The dragon that could destroy your body and soul in an instant? Maybe the dragon was destroyed by the accident. Maybe Dad would stop bellowing and throwing tantrums. I rolled down the window and let the wind sweep it all away. I was relieved that I wouldn't have to be near him.

Weeks later, doctors said Mom would never be the same; she would always have reduced lung capacity. It was late October when Dad went to drive Mom home from the hospital. The next morning, he took her to his mom's house, so he could go to work without worrying.

∾∾∾

Barb and I took turns going home every other weekend. When I returned home one early November weekend, everything looked the same. But when I entered the house an unfamiliar smell greeted me. Someone was cooking dinner! I rounded the corner to the kitchen. The table was set! Was it a holiday, I wondered? No. I was startled to find Mom at the stove stirring goulash.

"Welcome home," she said as she smiled and hugged me. Her hands were soft. Her hair was combed, not molded funny by a stocking cap.

"Hi, Mom," I managed to say, before dropping into a chair. "Smells good in here."

Did I have the right house? This was my mother? The only thing missing was an apron. My mother was a farmer; she loved being outdoors.

"How's school?" she asked.

"Well, I'm going to be on the 'A' honor roll. I'm getting ready to switch rooms. Ginnie's driving me crazy. At the end of the semester I'm moving in with Jan. She's on the ski team so she's not around much—that makes the room quiet. I like that."

"Maybe Ginnie needs you," Mom said quietly.

"Well, I don't need her. That's for sure!" I announced. Mom pulled up her stool to the sewing machine. The machine hummed as she patched Dad's jeans. Hauling my bag upstairs, I wondered, *Would she ever be able to be outside again, doing the things she loved? Had Dad changed?*

SLAYING THE MONSTER

- What behaviors did Teresa find unacceptable at home?
- Discuss domestic violence. Have you ever feared for your safety?
- What specific changes did Teresa undertake? Why? How?

MORE: DOMESTIC VIOLENCE INFORMATION

Domestic Violence is when one person in a relationship fails to treat the other person with respect. The abuser belittles, mocks, beats, pushes, hits, threatens, or the like. It can happen between a man and woman, domestic partners, siblings, boyfriend and girlfriend . . .

Typically, the abuser apologizes after the outburst, but repeats the behavior again, and again. Often domestic violence is connected to alcoholism, addictions, or what I call broken brain syndrome (mental/emotional illnesses, such as depression). *No one* deserves to be abused.

If this is happening to you call the national hotline now: 1-800-799-SAFE (7233) or 1-800-787-3224 (TTY). Tell your story. They can help you escape the situation and find healing. Website: www.ndvh.org.

Experiencing Domestic Violence is not a sign of a person's worth.

Assurance: God loves you, and created you to be respected. **You are a cherished child of God.** Genesis 1–2, Psalms 139, John 3:16

2

The Dragon's History

"TERESA, YOU HAVE A package!" exclaimed my dorm mate Roxy. "Thanks," I said and flew down the three flights of stairs and out the door to the mailroom. Jan tried to say hello on the sidewalk, but I galloped past her with a grin. "I've got a package!" I announced it to the world.

Taking the package I examined the return address; it was from my best friend. Gay! Art student that she was, she had doodled a crazy, cool piece of artwork in red ink for the address. She had even addressed it with her pet name for me, "Reesy!"

As I ripped open the package, a glow filled my heart. Crumpled newspaper, a sea green—almost turquoise—bandanna, and at the bottom, a book: *Our Bodies, Ourselves*, greeted me. I flopped down on my bed, and eagerly opened its newsprint pages. Wow! More information than I had ever seen about my physical body, women's issues, and emotions.

One of the chapters drew me up short: Domestic Violence. I had never heard of it. The book said no one had the right to hit you. No one had the right to belittle you, call you names, or threaten you. There was a name for such things—verbal, physical, and emotional abuse. Someone, somewhere else, had been where I had been! Tears streamed down my face as memories scrolled through my mind.

Calling card in hand, I dialed the hall phone, "Gay!"

When she heard my voice, I could tell she smiled, "Teresa! What's happening?"

"Thanks for the package, it's great," I said. "Where did you find the book? Have you read it?"

There was no pause in the conversation; we were on fast-forward, "Yeah, I read it. It's good, isn't it? My roommate has a copy of it. She let me read hers."

"Have you seen the chapter about my mom and dad?" My search was about to begin. Gay listened intently while I talked and talked. "It says that abuse travels down family lines. So the question is, where did it come from?" I hurried on, "I think I'll write to Mom's mom, Grandma Sweet, and ask her about her marriage."

ᖇ ᖇ ᖇ

"Hey, Gay!" I called out to her across the telephone lines.

"Hey yourself! What's up?" she responded. I could picture her sitting cross-legged on her bed.

"Grandma Sweet sent me a letter answering my questions. Want to hear it?" I asked.

"Sure. Go."

I unfolded the letter.

Dear Teresa,

If I answer all your questions, do you plan to write a book? Maybe I'll have a book written by the time I get them answered . . .

I paused to comment, "She goes on about a trip to Dubuque and what she saw. Okay, here's the rest of the letter."

You want to know about my marriage. Nothing, but work on the farm it seemed. Was O.K. otherwise. Loved my children very much. We wanted them to have it better than we did, so worked for that. There were times it was enjoyable, really. The part I didn't like was when he worked too hard, and nothing I would do pleased him. No, I didn't want to marry again [after he died.] No. I didn't want to farm. Married a town boy, never expected to farm. Five years later we were farming.

My dad farmed, so knew what it was. He was always home working. Forgot all my Swiss after Mother passed away, when I was twelve. To me he wasn't fascinating, he was just Dad! Is your dad fascinating? Hot coffee made him happy; cold coffee was very bad. Had to cook on an old cook stove winter and summer! I was a tomboy, not a cook. My two older sisters were the cooks. Yes. I was afraid of him; he was mostly a stern dad.

I'll bet you probably don't remember all the questions you asked me.

"She goes on with some other stuff. What do you think?" I asked. Gay was silent.

"It's a lot to take in," Gay said, finally.

"What sticks with me is where she says, 'The part I didn't like was when he worked too hard, and nothing I would do pleased him.' There's a pattern with Grandpa Sweet being difficult or impossible to please, and my dad being difficult or impossible to please. I didn't ask Grandma Sweet what Grandpa would do or say when he wasn't pleased."

"Oh my gosh!" Gay interrupted me. "I'm late for class. Gotta' go. Talk to you later. Bye. Love you."

I hung up the phone slowly. In my mind, I could hear my dad come in for supper.

"Ma, what'd you do today?" Dad asked. He gave Mom a long to-do list every morning.

"We took the nails out of that wagon load of salvaged boards, so we can use them to build the lean-to. The kids filled the tar buckets. Ready for you to do Henry's roof . . ." Mom gave him the full account.

"How come you didn't fix that fence or take out the load of manure?" Dad demanded. Nothing was ever done to Dad's satisfaction.

∾∾∾

Barb, my older sister, was connected! She knew my dad's father's sister. I wanted to get the *real* scoop on that side of the family.

Barb said, "Great Aunt Sis will be glad to see you."

I wasn't too sure that Aunt Sis would be glad to see me, but I went, pushed by my burning desire to know where the domestic abuse came from. Driving up in my Delta '88 Oldsmobile, I came to a stop beside the ranch-style house. When I rang the bell a small woman with dark eyes and zing in her manner swung open the door.

"Why, Teresa! Barb told me you'd stop by to visit me someday! It's good to see you," Aunt Sis exclaimed. She embraced me and flitted around me like a bird greeting a favorite mate. Then, I followed her to the old-fashioned kitchen. She was bustling around to find a sweet for us.

I took a deep breath and asked, "What was it like to come here from Switzerland?"

She was quiet. "Mother was so sick on the ship. I hadn't been out of the hospital too long myself. Oooh! We were all so seasick: Jay and I, Lew and Johann. When we finally got to the states they held us up at Ellis Island. We took the train to Wisconsin. Finally, we made it to Chicago. Dad met us at the depot. It was winter—ach, so cold." She shuddered before she went on, "There had been a thaw, so the roads were nothing but mud. When we got to the house, even our trunks were covered with mud.

"Oh my god, the house was nothing! It had no electricity. We had always had electricity in Switzerland. The roads in Switzerland were paved, no mud flying. The walls of the house—you could see through the cracks straight outdoors. Mother was so very sick. Ten days after we arrived, she died. Then things got rough. I had to thaw the bread in the stove, in the morning, before we could cut it for breakfast—it froze overnight sitting on the table.

"Dad was doing roadwork then, building bridges. He would come home with his paycheck and then drive out to town, and drink it away. Thankfully the neighbors took us under their wing. Mrs. Kate helped us with food and clothes, and then they hired Jay, your granddad. I was so homesick I would read the Swiss newspaper under the blankets at night! It used up precious kerosene oil, but it was all the connection I had." She paused. There was a far-away look in her eyes.

"Sometimes, I would go with Dad to town, and I would end up sitting on the curb while he drank away our grocery money. It was awful. If there wasn't any food, he would beat me. When we were out of flour, and he was heading to town, I would wait until he was in the wagon, driving off, before I would shout out what we needed.

"Finally, one night I ran away. There was a family some miles down the road. I thought I would go there, but on the way I stumbled and fell into a rock quarry and got soaking wet. They took me in. Of course, Dad knew where I was. He begged me to come home. At first, I said I would not come home. I was working for these people, and life was a little better. But he kept pleading with me and writing me letters. So I gave in.

"It wasn't long before he went back to his ways of drinking up the food money and beating me. So I ran away again. This time I did not go back home. I was twelve or thirteen. Lots of girls hired themselves out; then the money was sent home to their families," she concluded.

I sat wide-eyed at my great aunt's Formica kitchen table. Here was a part of the explanation for where the domestic violence had come from, all the way back to my great-grandfather.

Later, I called Barb. She had been helping me research the cause of this misery.

"Have you heard the news?" she asked me.

"What news?"

Barb rushed on, "Mom had her follow up tests to check her lung capacity and stuff. Remember how the doctors said she would never have full lung capacity again—too much scar tissue? The tests couldn't find any scar tissue! What a miracle."

"Wow!" I said with joy, before telling Barb about my visit to Great Aunt Sis.

Barb was silent; then said, "I called Dad's sister. Remember how we couldn't understand why no one intervened when we were kids? Dad's sister said we shouldn't be so hard on Dad; he had a rough childhood."

It was my turn to be silent. I was angry! One person's victimization justified another person's abuse?

"Exactly what was rough about his childhood?" I asked Barb. "About all I know is that Dad says during the Depression there was a year when all they ate was oatmeal."

Barb answered, "Remember Dad was nine years old when Grandpa Jay's thumb was taken off by a belt on the baler? Dad had to drive him to the hospital at the age of nine! How he could see over the dashboard, I don't know!"

"Yah," I said. "I remember how some of the farmers around home called Dad 'Little Jay.' It was because Grandpa Jay hired out to do work for all these farmers—corn picking, baling hay, and stuff. Dad had to go along to help him."

Barb went on, "When Grandpa lost his thumb he got gangrene and almost died."

"Oh, now I remember. Grandma Claire got pneumonia, went to the hospital and the kids were all 'farmed' out to the neighbors. The father of the family Dad stayed with was really stingy with food. I wonder if the neighbor was abusive."

"Dad talks about Uncle Cam, too. You know Uncle Cam was Grandma Claire's younger brother; he inherited the family farm. Every summer Dad or his brother would go and work on Uncle Cam's farm to earn money to pay for school clothes. They say Uncle Cam drank too much," Barb said.

"So what we're saying is our dad had to grow up fast, without much time to be a kid. But his sisters say Dad and his brothers were treated like little kings in the house," I said. We talked a while longer.

Hanging up the phone, I was reeling from the weight of it all. Piecing things together was difficult and painful.

SLAYING THE MONSTER

- What resources have you found helpful when it comes to learning about your mind and body?

- Name the patterns Teresa uncovered. Reflect on the patterns in your extended family.

- Why did Teresa question relatives about the past?

- Share your experiences of having been hurt, hurting others, or helping others.

MORE: THE ORIGINS OF DOMESTIC VIOLENCE

Where Does Abuse Come From? Figuring it out often involves tracing the patterns of past generation's behavior. Most people do not intend to grow up and abuse others. However, many who were abused as children become abusive.

There is Data that alcoholism and domestic violence are ways that people act out or self-medicate when they are depressed. I call depression 'broken brain'; psychiatrists call it "chemical imbalance" and "mental or emotional illness." When serotonin or dopamine is lacking in our brain we may lack the ability to control our actions even though we desperately want to change our behavior. Depression is now known to be hereditary. More details can be found in the book, *A Relentless Hope* by Gary Nelson.

The World is an Imperfect Place; we are human, not God. This means: we make mistakes, we have free will, and we are prone to illnesses of the body and mind.

Assurance: Jesus did not come into the world to condemn us for our bad behavior or brokenness (John 3:17).

3

Free Fall

MY MANIC APPROACH TO life as a college freshman had been incredible. It was as sweet as the strawberry daiquiris and ice cream grasshoppers I had tried for the first time. Rooming with Jan was a blast. Her parents came and took us out to an incredible restaurant—in a railroad boxcar. I felt like an alien beamed onto another planet.

By February the antics of going out on Friday nights had dulled, and the regularity with which some of my friends drank and got sick, baffled me. I had decided I wanted a real relationship with my dad. I sent him a letter telling him everything I was grateful for that he had said and done. I thanked him for having been a patient teacher, a regular presence, a good neighbor, a kind dad when we were sick, a tough guy who never quit, an incredible risk-taker, and more.

I heard nothing back.

Hans, a youth director I had met on a mission trip, wrote to me and invited me to be part of a youth lay witness program at University of Wisconsin-Oshkosh. I took him up on the offer. It was great to see old friends from the mission trip, powerful too. You could feel the Holy Spirit present in the room. It was like a bee buzzing around everywhere, or a warm, warm breeze. Inside it felt like drinking brandy—everything begins to glow warm from your insides out.

Second semester continued on and the glow began to fade.

"I don't know what it is," I told my friend, Donna, from across the hall. "I feel totally unsettled. Something isn't right. Vocational Rehabilitation doesn't seem like the right major for me. "Hmm," Donna responded thoughtfully. "Tell me more about it."

I told her of my frustrations and went on to talk about the coming summer. "I refuse to go back to my hometown and live with Mom and

Dad. That would be a nightmare," I said aloud. "I'm going to look around for summer jobs that provide housing."

I applied for a summer job at a church camp doing maintenance work. Ben, a sixty-something-year-old man, was the camp manager.

He called me, "Teresa, we don't hire girls to do maintenance work, but you could be a kitchen girl. They serve food, wash the dishes and clean the cabins at the end of the week after the campers go home."

"Oh," I said and politely responded, "I'll have to get back to you." I was angry! He didn't know who I was. Told me girls couldn't do outside work, repair things, and mow the lawn with tractors. Humph.

But I took the job; it meant I wouldn't have to live at home. The good news was that kitchen girls got afternoons off! I could swim in the lake and sunbathe. The maintenance guys worked from eight to five with little break time for fun. The pay was lousy, but I was sticking to my vow that I would never again live at home.

Nature had always been a sanctuary for me. I sang and praised God while riding my bike, and prayed while swimming. I tried fasting for the first time in my life. I'd decided to go twenty-four hours without food. I found it impossible to get to sleep; my friend Lynne rubbed my back and tried to soothe me.

I wrote letters to a bunch of people, including Hans and another youth counselor. Their mentoring and affirmation meant the world to me. Few men had ever affirmed me. I felt that other than my Grandma Sweet and my mom, no adult had ever unconditionally approved of me. But they were my grandmother and my mother, didn't they have to love me unconditionally?

Besides, this was male approval. My upbringing said that a man's opinion counted more than a woman's any day of the week.

ଊଊଊ

Truckers! Who noticed them? Who cared? I wondered as I zoomed toward my sophomore year in college. I was focused on figuring out a new major. Moving in was good, but not the blast of the previous year. Jan, Rita, and I were rooming together in a co-ed dorm. Only trouble was, I felt uncomfortable around men. No longer was the whole floor of my dorm a safe haven and a place to bounce from room to room. My vow of "things being different" was slipping.

Females? I could act my way into believing I was equal. Men? No way. I was scared. Scared of being with them—what if they were like my dad? Scared of getting too close—safety for me meant never fully trusting a man. Scared of being alone—single women were "old maids" and didn't count in life. I was going to count if it was the last thing I did.

Then again, I was desperate for approval and romance. Everyone mattered to someone, but I believed I mattered to no one. I was a bird without a home, wheeling and searching. A guy named D.J. had written to me all summer, nothing but light chitchat. I wrote letters back to him saying nothing. Back at school, a couple of dates with skinny, boyish-looking, D.J. was all it took.

"Come on, Teresa, let's go back to my room," he said. But once in the room he only seemed interested in getting to second base; I was interested in getting far away.

"Sorry, D. J., I've got to go," I said, as I extracted myself from his wandering hands. That was the end of D.J. and me.

$$\sim\sim\sim$$

School was good, but it didn't feel like I was in the right place anymore. The euphoria of independence was gone and in its place was emptiness. I was taking a Vocational Rehabilitation Internship. God had created me with a deep desire to help people. At the Sheltered Workshop, I was assigned to work with a gentle, elderly man who was severely retarded. I started by assessing his abilities.

"Eddie!" I said with a warm, cheerful confidence I did not feel, "Let's count pennies." I tried to give him a start by saying, "One …"

He said nothing. I jotted down on my paper that maybe counting could be an objective. Or would that be a goal? A glance through his file made it clear that he had never been taught how to cross the street using the crosswalk and the walk light. In the dim light of the old building, I sat at the battle-scarred and wounded table writing up my objectives and goals. Even it seemed depressed.

Week after week I pulled pennies out of my pocket and wound up my smile like one would screw a light bulb into the socket. "Look, Eddie, do you see the picture of the person walking?" I pointed to the light post on the opposite side of the street. He didn't respond.

Week after week I wrote words that gathered dust and glumness in his file. The leaves had withered and blown off the trees. My confidence that Vocational Rehabilitation was the right choice was gone, left with the leaves—ground underfoot and slumped in the gutter.

Week after week Rita and I would go for nightly walks after dinner or homework.

Friday nights, Rita and Jan urged me, "Come on, let's go out."

"No thanks," I would murmur and slide down onto the floor to write letters and study my mail. I spread out University of Wisconsin brochures and majors. I planned my weekends. First, I would drive to the University of Wisconsin-Eau Claire. Then I would look at the University of Wisconsin-La Crosse. Trouble was, I didn't know what I was looking for; I only knew I wanted to be in a helping profession. I prayed for clarity. I prayed and prayed. No peace.

Nursing became a last resort. Wasn't it the ultimate helping profession?

At mid-semester I told Jan and Rita, "Well, guys, it looks like I am going to transfer to the University of Wisconsin-Milwaukee this January."

"What?" Jan exclaimed.

"Are you sure?" Rita asked me.

Maybe this would get me out of my funk; it was my secret hope. Before I even had a chance to apply for housing, I got a letter from Hans.

ოოო

Dear Teresa,

I have this great idea! Why don't you live with us while you attend UW Milwaukee? Janet and I would love to have you come. We could give you your own room and board, if you could contribute a hundred dollars a month to the household. What do you think?

Yours truly,
Hans

ოოო

Sitting at my desk with my dancing hippo mug and typewriter, I stared at the letter. I did not see the real words. I saw subliminal messages: You are wanted. This is the financial deal/steal of a lifetime. Save big money at Hans's! You have a safe place! Little did I know my Dr. Jekyll/Mr. Hyde journey was scheduled to begin in two months.

While home for a little while over Christmas break I wandered around in a fog. What had I done? I'd left behind healthy, good friendships and was moving to a place where I had to start over.

I hung out at the Dance Club with old friends. We danced. I drank my signature drink: ice water. I saw Don! He was at the corner of the bar.

He looked at me appreciatively between taking shots at the pool table and said, "You're back," in a welcoming tone.

We had dated some a year before. His wide shoulders and gray eyes spoke to me. Sitting with Don's arm around me, I felt wonderful. Before I had left for college, he had asked me to move in with him. I had been enchanted and anguished by turns. I knew Grandma Sweet would not approve. I could not bear to disappoint her or to trust any man. Now I was enchanted, all over again.

∾ ∾ ∾

January blew through with plenty of snow; I stamped my boots off before I carried my stuff into my room at Hans's house. His young kids wound around my legs with curiosity and laughter. Acceptance was in the air. Good food was on the table. I thought it would be all right.

School was another story. Gut gripped by fear, I stumbled from building to strange building looking for my biology classroom. It was a vast lecture hall; I felt lost and tongue-tied. I was back to my high school loner status. Invisible. No one invited me to lunch. I sat in a dark lounge with gritty music and ate my grapefruit, sour section by section.

During the fourth week of chemistry class my lab mate asked, "Do you understand this stuff?"

I shook my head.

"We can try it this way," she said. I went along with her.

"Teresa." The Teacher's Aid handed back my quiz. The grade was a big black "D."

"How did you do?" I asked my lab mate. She held up her matching "D." "Come on. Let's go ask the T.A.," I said.

My stomach knotted up at the idea of asking for help. His attitude was, "I'm in the PhD program, busy and important." It radiated from him like the stench of a skunk.

"We need help with this past week's quiz. We don't understand the concepts." The guy's blonde hair was a bit disheveled, but there was nothing unclear about his words.

Clipping the words precisely he said, "If you didn't understand last week's lesson, there's no way I can explain this week's lesson to you." I was a sinking stone and my G.P.A. was going down with me.

Back at Hans and Janet's over dinner I was asked, "So, how was your day?"

I shrugged, "Fine." I turned with a pretend smile on my face and asked their little boys, "What kind of truck do you like best? Fire engines, or dump trucks?"

Hans said, "Teresa, come and join my college group, at the church."

I went reluctantly.

"Hey, Hans! Why did the chicken cross the road?" some guy called out to Hans when we got there. A quiet guy named Donnie sat playing his guitar in the corner. Eileen, with the wire-rim glasses was pre-med. Wow! She must be really smart. They all seemed relaxed and confident. I went home engulfed in a growing inferiority complex.

∾∾∾

The phone rang—it was Don! Don never called. I was excited.

"Don! What's up?"

"I have a proposition to make ..." he told me all about it. Wow! I must really matter to him. He went on with the idea, "so the upshot is I need a couple thousand dollars to start it and I wondered if you could loan me the money."

My heart fell. "You need money?! You called me to ask for money?" I asked. My voice rose.

"What kind of a proposition did you think I was going to make?" he asked evenly.

"I thought ... I thought ..." I had trouble forming the words. "I thought you were calling because you liked me, because you missed me." There was silence.

"So you thought ..." he began.

I interrupted and said with a rush, "I thought you cared. I thought someday-you-might-ask-me-to-marry-you."

Slowly his answer came across the phone lines, "No. No, it's not like that."

In my room, I yanked open my journal. As the tears dripped onto the page, I squeezed out the words of anger.

You knew better, Teresa. You knew better than to think a guy would want to marry you. You are too mouthy, too bossy, too ugly, too mean, and too unfeminine. You knew better. You fantasized. How could you be so dumb? How could you have confused kisses with caring? Stupid girl. Stupid, just plain stupid.

I rolled off the bed and slid a package out of the closet. I had been putting together a birthday package for Rita. There, in the shoebox was a gigantic Hershey bar. I ripped open the paper and foil. But there was no joy in that chocolate bar.

The M*A*S*H theme song was on the TV in the den, "Suicide is painless. It brings on many changes …" Hans was out there unwinding from youth group.

I stumbled out into the den and slumped on the carpeting near the recliner. He was lying on the old couch in his white tee shirt and jeans watching the little TV. Janet and the boys had headed to bed before nine, like every night. I reached out for Mac, the dog, and held on to him as if I were holding on for dear life.

"What's going on?" Hans asked when he saw my red eyes. He swept his blonde hair out of his eyes and across his bald spot, then adjusted his wire rims. He sat up; his Buddha-like belly sat up on its own.

"I don't want to live," the words came like teardrops. Hans sat in the den with me for hours until I decided to live through another day.

❧ ❧ ❧

Every day I dragged myself out of bed and drove the half-hour to school. To avoid paying the parking fees, I walked the mile or so from my car to the school. On the way I jumped over snow-clogged sidewalks.

Sometimes I sang while walking. With the sun shining, my breath frozen in the air—it was the one moment I was glad to be alive. "Sunshine, on my shoulders, makes me happy."

Some nights I called my sister.

"Barb," I would say glumly into the phone.

"Hey you!" she would say back. It seemed like she was my only friend.

❧ ❧ ❧

One night the M*A*S*H late night song had begun when Hans asked me a strange question, "Am I a father figure to you?"

Startled. Confused.

"No. No!" No, he was no father figure to me. Fathers were tyrants and unpredictable. "Of course not," I said.

✶✶✶

The M*A*S*H routine stuck. First, I took Mac for a short run and a cool down walk in the starry night, then watched TV until midnight with Hans.

In mid-February, Hans reached out and began stroking my fingers as I sat in the recliner with my arm on the armrest. He didn't look at me. He said nothing. I sat paralyzed. It was like it wasn't happening; but it was. I was suddenly very alone.

Perhaps the only words he spoke were, "Come over here." Hans beckoned me to come and lie with him on the couch. Startled, I obeyed. I was so deeply depressed, so far removed from reality, nothing seemed real. Hans was eager to touch me. I was disgusted by his giant belly and lack of handsomeness. But I was dying inside of loneliness and depression. I told no one. Who would have believed me?

There was no safe place. He was my landlord. I was ashamed. I had always said he was wonderful. Would I go back on my word? How could this have happened? This was the person who had taught me to always keep your office door open when the opposite sex was with you in order to avoid even the appearance of impropriety.

I didn't know how to tell my parents—things we had never talked about in our eighteen years together. Besides, what good would that do? Living back at my parents' house would be a nightmare. During the day there was this guy I knew who was a youth director, a mentor, a father to his children, a husband to his wife, and a spiritual guide. Dr. Jekyll. At night, there was this silent guy who touched me and touched me and kissed me. Mr. Hyde.

✶✶✶

In early April, Barb asked me, "Do you want to go motorcycle shopping with me?"

"Yes! Yes!" Here was something that would get me out of the house. Here was freedom and familiarity. Barb and I had grown up riding motorcycles year round to our part-time jobs.

It stood on the sparkling floor of the shop—a sleek, black 440 Kawasaki. New! Its siren song was strong. Immediately I was drawn to it. Drawn to what it represented. If there was an escape, this was it. If there was a way to declare independence, this was it. When I rode it; it was like flying free. I bought it.

෴෴෴

Hans responded in shock, "You bought what? You can't drive that on these interstates. It isn't safe."

I smiled smugly. And he didn't want to be my father figure! Humph. But when I said, "I'm dropping out of school," he took action.

"Come with me." He drove me straight to his alma mater. He walked me to the admissions office. The application in hand, he said, "Fill it out. It can't hurt." Like always, I did what he said.

෴෴෴

Spring snapped at my back, playfully, as I rode from Hans's house toward my hometown, defeated and determined at the same time. My grand new leather jacket with the perfect Darth Vader helmet gave me power. I would get a job. I went to Grandma Sweet's house.

Going in the side door I called out, "Hellooo! It's Teresa."

Her voice came from beyond the kitchen, "In here."

When I turned the corner into the living room, she broke into a smile and stood up.

"Hello, Sweetiepie." Her soft hands with beautiful fingernails cupped my face and she hugged me. "Do you want something to eat? I have some bars on the counter."

"Thanks, Grandma!" I spun around and was back in a flash with a blondie brownie in hand. The chewy nuts and chocolate chips combined to form love in my mouth. I plopped down on the couch.

"How are you?" she asked.

I swallowed hard. "I'm okay." She could tell I wasn't okay.

"What's wrong?"

"I don't know what to do. I don't know what I want to do with my life. Nursing isn't it. Chemistry is awful. I don't get it. I think I'll quit college and get a job."

"You are going to be all right," she assured me. She hugged me again, and I headed home.

"Hellooo!" I called out when I went in Mom and Dad's house. There was an echo. An early fly buzzed in the sunshine of the window over the kitchen sink as I filled a glass with water. Dumping my glass on top of the heap of breakfast dishes, I looked up at the clock. It was three o' clock. Hmm. Mom must be in the field disking.

I went outside and waded through the knee-high grass behind the barn to check the north field. No, not there. I climbed onto the motorcycle and flew over the hills with great joy. I saw the tractor rounding the corner. When Mom made the wide corner with the big red and white Heston tractor, she saw me pulling into the field's gate. I waved as she pulled to a stop. Climbing the steps I opened the narrow door and propped myself halfway on the seat arm.

"How are you?" she said breaking into a smile. Her whole face lit up. She was the picture of home. Her short hair had been churned by the wind and her tanned face kissed by the spring sun. Mom put it into gear and began the next round, breaking up the plowed alfalfa with the steel disks, smoothing it for planting.

"I think I'm going to quit school," I said.

She didn't react, just drove on calmly.

"I don't know what I want to do with my life. I'm a failure at chemistry, so nursing is out." The dust billowed behind the disk. White puffy clouds were stitched peacefully across the blue, blue Wisconsin skies. She listened.

"I think I'll go apply for some jobs in town."

"All right, if that's what you want to do," she answered. Slowing down to let me out, she turned near my bike.

"I'll see you at suppertime!" I called out, as she pulled away for the next lap. Before I could mount the cycle, she was halfway down the field.

McDonald's, Pizza Hut, Kmart: I went down the street where all the stores gathered and filled out applications, then on a whim took the short bypass to the lumber yard. It was like a second home to our family. I had spent hours there as a teenager, picking up lumber for Dad. I applied to load trucks.

With his mashed cap framing his weathered face, Eric grinned and said, "You're hired!" As the foreman of the yard he had watched me grow up loading bundles of shingles and lumber with his yard workers. It was well known that Dad worked us hard.

"I can't start until school's out," I responded. Heading home, I felt like I was drowning in a sea of sorrow and defeat. Come back and live here, with Mom and Dad? No way. Rent an apartment? How much was that going to cost me?

☙☙☙

My last month on campus I found joy in the lake breezes that came dancing up the hill; my escape from the sexual abuse, guilt, and shame was around the corner. The sun warmed my empty bones, and I was relieved to find out that Carroll College would accept me before they received this semester's grades. Whew! Maybe I would go back to school. First though, I had to find a way to make it through the summer.

That same week I received a letter in the mailbox.

> *Dear Teresa,*
>
> *I was reading the Wisconsin Conference UMC newspaper and saw this. I thought you might be interested.*
>
> *Love,*
Grandma S.

Enclosed was a clipping, advertising summer ministry internships for students: housing, and food provided, as well as a $1,500 stipend! Wow. I could do that with my eyes closed. I sent in my resume and continued trudging to classes.

Within a few weeks I had the answer! I sent Grandma a great thank-you note. I would be living halfway between home and Milwaukee, working with a pastor who served three little churches. On my way to the interview, I followed the road curving this way around young corn and then that way past woodlands flooded with blue-lavender bluebells. I began to feel alive again. Confident on the outside, shattered shards inside, I rode my way toward reinventing myself.

SLAYING THE MONSTER

- What did Teresa do to remove herself from the situation?
- Have you, or people you know, faced similar situations?
- Is your home, or workplace, a safe place?
- If not, what can you do, who can you turn to for help?
- If you know someone who has been or is being sexually abused what can you do to support them?

MORE: SEXUAL ABUSE INFORMATION

Sexual Abuse occurs when one person with power over another, engages in sexual behavior. Power comes from the position you have (pastor, parent, adult, boss). If you have the power, or authority over the person's freedom, lodging, spiritual care, finances, etc. and you engage in sexual behavior with that person, it can be defined as sexual abuse.

If You Are Being Sexually Abused, or Have Been Assaulted, please call the National Sexual Assault Hotline: 1.800.656.HOPE; Website: www .RAINN.org

But, We Are Both Adults! This may be true, but it does not remove the power imbalance. If you want to be in a relationship (sexual or otherwise) with someone, in order to create equality you need the person to be free of their power over you. ie. Find a different job, apartment . . .

What's a Sexual Predator? It is someone who seeks out emotionally vulnerable people, and uses their power over them to engage in sexual acts which constitute abuse.

Sexuality is a Gift from God given to each of us. God created us male and female in God's own image. Sacred. Holy. Good. When sexuality is expressed between two people within the bounds of commitment it is a good and right thing (trust building, and enormously pleasurable too!) When sexual behavior occurs outside the bounds of commitment, there is tremendous risk to your psyche. One resource regarding sexuality as a gift is the website: www.americancatholic .org/Newsletters/YU/ay0801.asp

More Information about sexual abuse and healing, given by leading expert, Dr. Marie Fortune, can be found at: www.faithtrustinstitute .org. Her books are excellent.

Assurance: Psalm 139, Genesis 1, 2, 1 Corinthians 7, 1 Thessalonians 4:3

4

A Baby Step Toward Healing

"HELLO, YOU MUST BE Teresa," the red-haired lady with porcelain skin said with great verve. She smiled in a grand fashion, making quite a picture in her white pants suit, which showed off her slender figure.

"Yes," I responded timidly.

"I'm Pastor Lu. You can call me Lu. Let me show you around this church." After seeing the sanctuary with its pews marching up toward the altar, then descending to the church basement complete with tables eerily echoing long-gone potlucks, we settled into her office.

I didn't need to say anything. She was busily explaining everything, from the way that she preached at the three churches, to the people who were a real inspiration to her. She was like a songbird—fresh from a night's sleep—singing and singing with glee. Back in the office after the tour, I remembered to smooth out my skirt before I sat down.

"You'll be living with the Southerlys on their farm, west of here. They're longtime members of Pleasant Valley, and their children are all grown. You'll be eating suppers at some of the homes of the folks around here, at Hebron Church.

"The services are all on Sunday morning, one at nine a.m., one at ten a.m., and one at eleven a.m. You'll be accompanying me on the circuit every Sunday, reading Scripture and leading prayer. I'll have you preach once toward the end of the ten weeks. We'll do some visitation together. Then, you'll do some of the visitation to shut-ins alone. You'll be assisting with Bible study, Vacation Bible School, as well as attending the Golden Agers lunches, the Administrative Council meetings, and church picnics. Do you have any questions for me?"

"Not that I can think of right now." I said, trying to take it all in.

"See you June first!" she said as she cheerily strode toward the parsonage, which was held in the embrace of the church grounds.

I was like a kite that had been wrapped up in a cold, dark garage for the winter, trampled on by people searching for snow shovels and sleds. But spring had sprung; chemistry was done. Back at Hans and Janet's house I placed their house key on the table, relieved no one was home. After I bungee-corded my remaining stuff to the cycle, I flew away, soaring on the updrafts of hope.

❧ ❧ ❧

By mid-June, I was getting to know Lu.

"I really get a charge out of seeing Michelle. She's so upbeat. But, I tell you what, Juanita gets to me every time!"

I listened, but didn't understand.

"It's so lonely here," she remarked as she took a tight turn on a back road. "I miss being able to get to the store, or see my friends, without having to drive more than thirty minutes."

For the first time, I really began to listen to the sermons. Before, sermons had seemed like a few crumbs tossed out to give you a vague idea of a trail to God, but with Lu (and with riding the circuit, listening to her preach the same thing three times in a row) all that changed. She preached about a Jesus who was personal and shaped her. Pastor Lu shared how I could be shaped too. Her sermons met me where I was, in the midst of my secret shame and misery.

Wise Lu's knowing eyes must have seen my deep wounds, heard the brokenness rattling brittle and unmended inside. But she stepped into my life only as far as I welcomed her. No further.

Each day, I rode my cycle to the church office, pulled a skirt out of my backpack and changed in the bathroom. In Lu's tiny blue car, we swept across counties to visit people at the hospital in one city and a nursing home in a separate place. Then, gradually, she gave me lists of people I should call and go visit. Every weeknight, families from the church alternated having me over for supper.

A tall, buxom farmer's wife named Velma invited me to supper. It was no secret she hoped to match her son up with me. Junior came in the door. Farmer tan, lank hair, slow talking—not my type at all. I tried to be polite to this guy who moved at puddle speed, and hedged off his mother's hinting. The dinner table was filled with sliced tomatoes and cucumbers with ham and scalloped potatoes. The smell made my mouth water. As soon as it was polite, I stood up.

"Thank you so much for the delicious meal," I smiled. Nodding at Junior, I said, "Nice to meet you."

With great thankfulness, I revved up my cycle and crunched down the driveway, enjoying the gentle breeze that swayed the Queen Anne's lace in the ditches and made the milkweed pods dance on the banks.

∾ ∾ ∾

In the afternoons, if there was time, I would get on my bicycle and fly around the country roads trying to spin the awful secrets out of my head. I'd return home to journal and weep, falling asleep in the early evening. I could not cry enough to get the winter's tragedy out of my system. Still I didn't tell anyone. Who would believe me?

∾ ∾ ∾

The end of the summer rolled around; it was humid and hot. Leaves curled in self-defense. The Queen Anne's lace was clothed in soft, tan-colored dust. Not one of the three churches had air conditioning, just arched windows and paper funeral-home fans

The ten weeks were over; I was to preach the final sermon. For days I had read the passage over and over trying to see what the disciples saw, smell the fish cooking, and hear the bystanders murmuring. Searching the dry commentary pages in the church office I had found inspiration and a generous share of five syllable words.

∾ ∾ ∾

Facing the first service crowd at Hebron, I found my tongue dry and stumbled over ordinary words. My stomach rolled and pitched, like I was at sea on a rough day. Here were the people I had come to know; ladies in their sandals, and men in slacks—their foreheads white from wearing a hat all summer. The flowers on the altar gave off their summer lily scent.

I arrived as they sang the opening hymn of the service at Siloam. The small friendly crowd, with the pianist fumbling over the keys, felt homey and safe to me. Preaching was easier here. Climbing into the car during Siloam's last hymn, I believed that the last service of the morning would go equally smoothly.

Lu pulled the car up sharply at the back of Pleasant Valley; we slipped inside during their first hymn; my eyes roved the aisles noting Julie's smiling eyes. At eight years old, she shimmered. Her grandmother was in the pew with her. Row upon row of familiar faces greeted my searching eyes. But then, my eyes stopped in disbelief and dismay. It couldn't be.

It couldn't be. There was my dad, with his thick hair combed back 1950s style, along with Mom and Grandma Sweet. Sitting next to them were all of my brothers and sisters. The whole family had showed up!

My dad had never come to an event I was in—not the junior high church musical or the live nativity scene at Christmas. He had never visited the church camp where I worked or the colleges I attended. Nervous took on a whole new meaning.

The sermon came and went. The service ended with the regular benediction and I walked down the aisle with Pastor Lu to the front door. There we greeted people as they exited.

"You are a fine preacher, Teresa!"

"What a gift you have been to us."

"Thank you for the sermon."

The last person out was my dad. Dad stood there, in his dress shoes that only saw action a few times a year, with tears cradled in his eyes. He hugged me tightly for the blink of an eye. Then in a hoarse, unfamiliar voice he said, "I'm proud of you, kid."

With tears welling up in my own eyes, the humid heat of summer immersing me, and my family milling around me, we went to enjoy the farewell picnic.

Pie and ice cream, cake and watermelon, brownies and fruit salad filled the dessert table. As the speeches were made and the flies swatted, I heard a buzzing noise. It wasn't the flies, or the odd bee passing through. It was the commotion filling me up to overflowing, and drowning me in a love and acceptance I had not experienced before. For a farewell present I was given a suitcase! Never had I owned a suitcase. I strapped it to my motorcycle and as I rode off the Holy Spirit murmured to me, "You can do this. I flow through you."

I said to myself, I *could* do this. But I didn't want to be a preacher.

~~~

Several weeks later, I found myself riding up to Carroll College on my motorcycle with a duffel bag. Students were talking a mile a minute, moving in and about, greeting old friends with high fives and hugs. Me? I was a stranger in a strange land again.

September's crispness was filled with glee. Taking the stairs two at a time I moved swiftly down the hall looking for my room. I stood at the window in my new room with the clamber of voices washing over me from the hallway; in front of me stretched out the campus and my future.

The summer had given me new confidence. The depth of last winter's depression had mostly faded. Pausing in the restroom next to the row of sinks, a woman with wavy hair introduced herself to me.

"I'm Jean. Oh, you're new here? Who's your roommate?"

"Briana," I answered.

"You're going to like her; she's a nice black girl," Jean said as she exited the opposite door. Startled, I headed back to my room. I didn't have time to think it over; there stood Briana and her family. I had never been introduced to an African American person before now. Briana and I had exchanged letters with each other, but . . . I was relatively inexperienced in the area of the world's diversity. In my hometown, there were only two kids I knew who weren't of European descent. The girl from Persia was bright and fun. The girl from China was calm and a friend of mine.

A native of Wyoming, Briana was pre-med. That alone awed me. Beyond her brown skin and glossy hair, she was lit by an inner peace. Briana's parents were immediately lovable.

"Ready for lunch?" Briana asked.

I nodded and we headed to the cafeteria. Taking my tray I followed her as we wove around the tables. She sat down with her other African-American friends in the dining hall, and I sat with her. I was puzzled by the way the cafeteria was split by race, African Americans at a table or two, whites at all the others.

༺ ༺ ༺

"Teresa, my job is to help you get credit for the courses you completed at other colleges," my advisor said. When my previous course titles did not match any of the courses at Carroll, he instructed me to "Bring in your term papers, class syllabi, and book lists, so I can match up them up with similar courses here."

Back at the dorm, I exclaimed, "Briana, you won't believe it! My advisor managed to transfer every one of my credits. It's nothing less than a miracle."

❧❧❧

Sundays, I attended the same church as I had the previous year. Hans was still the youth director there.

"Teresa, I believe you are called to be a minister," Hans said, with his feet kicked back on the desk.

He echoed what Lu had said when she took me out for pie the week before.

Lu had leaned across the table and said, "Have you been praying about it? God is calling you to be an ordained minister."

With Hans and Lu tag-teaming me, my junior year passed. I had pushed the sexual abuse to a dark corner of my brain. But I was on guard all the time.

❧❧❧

As my senior year took shape, I began to spiral downward emotionally. I spent huge amounts of time in prayer trying to determine what it was I was supposed to do with my life.

"Teresa," Briana said to me as we shared a Twix candy bar, "If God is calling you to be a pastor, you should follow the call."

Dan, a pre-ministerial student, echoed Briana. "Do it. Take up the cross and follow Christ. You won't be sorry. I think you're called to be an ordained minister," Dan urged me. But I was convinced I was not worthy, not smart enough—not that I told anyone that.

Finally, I laid out a fleece. In the Bible, God calls Gideon to lead His people into battle. Gideon is afraid and doesn't want to do it. He asks God for a sign. He places a sheep's fleece on the ground and prays that if God is serious about this call, in the morning dew will cover the ground, but the fleece will be dry. In the morning Gideon sees that God answered exactly as he had prayed (Judges 6:33).

That night in my dorm room, I pulled my comforter up to my chin and prayed.

> *Dear God, you know me. You made me. I don't know what to do with my life. Almost everyone I know says I am called to ministry—to be an ordained minister in the United Methodist Church. Are you calling me?*
>
> *I'll know if you are calling me if I am admitted to Candler with a full scholarship. You know I don't have the money to attend seminary. You know Candler is best suited for my skills. You know I don't think I am graduate-school material. You know me. I wait for your sign. Amen.*

I sent in an application to Candler School of Theology at Emory University in Atlanta, Georgia. As the semester wore away, I tried to keep up with my studies and work on my final paper. Then one day the phone rang, interrupting my writing.

"This is Candler School of Theology calling. Is Teresa there?"

"This is she," I responded, wondering what was wrong now.

"We are missing your reference letter. We need you to send it in order for us to consider your application."

"I don't understand. I sent the first one a month ago. When you didn't receive it, I sent a second one, registered mail." I tried to blow off my disgust. "Okay. I'll send it again. Thank you." I said, with no real sincerity. I hung up, then dialed the phone.

"Good afternoon. How may I help you?" a kind voice inquired.

"Is Hans in?" I asked.

"Yes, he is. Hold on just a moment."

"Teresa!" Hans's enthusiasm vibrated the phone line. "What's up?"

"I need you to write another reference letter. They lost it."

"No problem."

"It is a problem. This is crazy. I'm tired of it," I moaned.

"I'll write the letter and take it to the post office right away," he assured me. I hung up, certain that this seminary thing was going to be a dead end. After all, how could God possibly want me—me who couldn't do anything right—to be a pastor? What would I do after I graduated if I didn't go to seminary?

༄ ༄ ༄

Weeks went by. I followed my routine. Penny, a friend from down the hall, and I went swimming at nine o'clock in the evenings. Walking across the cold campus with damp hair one night, I felt momentarily awake. I groaned out loud, "I have this final paper due and I feel like I'm going in circles."

Always good natured, Penny joined in, "I know what you mean; I have some papers due too."

I headed to my room. It was after ten o'clock. The smell of chlorine hovered around me as I wrestled with the door lock.

Ringgg, rinnggg. The lock gave way, and I raced to answer the phone.

"Hello?" I answered breathlessly.

"Hello," the energetic voice resounded over the phone, "Is this Teresa? This is Dean Nichols from Candler School of Theology."

"Yes, this is she," I said with great hesitancy. Was this it? The big "No"?

"Teresa, you have been accepted to be part of the incoming class of 1985 here at Candler School of Theology. You will be receiving a Sherman Scholarship. Welcome to Candler School of Theology!"

I slid down the wall. "Thank you," I said softly and hung up the phone. There in my purple sweatpants and damp tee shirt, I wailed to God. "Noooooooo. God, do you really mean this? What if I can't do it? How will I do this? Are you sure?" Wiping away the tears with my sleeve, I picked up my notebook and began to journal.

> *I never expected this to happen. What do I do now? A full scholarship! My grades are okay—maybe a B-plus average, but that's nothing great. Why do they want me? What am I going to do? On the other hand, Wow! I get to leave town, explore some other culture and get paid to go to school. That's a real deal.*
>
> *I know your Holy Spirit works through me, flows through me. I will go if you send me.*

"Hello," Hans's voice came on the line.

"I got in. I've been accepted!"

"Great! That's great, Teresa," Hans enthused and immediately began to give advice. "Make sure and study Evangelism with George Morris while you are there. And whatever you do, don't marry a man who is a pastor. Clergy couples are nothing but bad news . . ."

When he finally stopped to take a breath, I ended the conversation.

Walking across campus, I mulled over what he had said. What crazy remarks! Everyone I knew was already married, or engaged. I was already twenty-two years old. His advice was irrelevant to me. I was never getting married or having kids. I was convinced I'd be a horrible wife, and if marriage was what my parents had, I wanted no part of it.

SLAYING THE MONSTER

- What tragedies did Teresa face? Talk about the tragedies in your life.

- What did she do with the tragedy/sexual abuse?

- How did she begin to heal? Who showed her unconditional love?

- Have you asked God to guide you, call you for a special purpose?
- What happened, or is happening, because you have asked for God's direction? Is God speaking to you through others?

MORE: HOW I BEGAN TO HEAL

Begin to Heal from Tragedy

- Surround yourself with positive, upbeat, supportive people.
- Do *something*, work, or volunteer–it gives you a sense of self-worth.
- Tell someone else about the tragedy, in the telling you'll find you're not alone.
- If the person you tell dismisses you or belittles you, know that they don't have the ability to support you or give you what you need–call the hotlines listed at the end of chapter two for support.

Believe: God can take any event and use it for good, as long as we give the event to God and trust in God's guidance. Surround yourself with other believers who will uphold you and model ways to holiness and wholeness (Romans 8).

Assurance: Remember, you are loved. God has many traits and facets, but one of the most important traits of God is love (1 Corinthians 13). Jesus was sent to tell the world you are loved! (John. 3:16) You are loved.

5

Leaps of Faith

Aᴜɢᴜsᴛ 1985. Tʜᴇ ʜᴇᴀᴠʏ smell of pine and rolling hills welcomed me to Candler School of Theology. In the Candler courtyard, students moved to and fro, some with purpose, while others like me looked lost.

Juan was a new student, too. We were hanging out one sky blue day.

"Hey, you want to go to the mall?" he asked.

"Okay." I didn't have anything better to do than kill time. We walked to his car. I buckled up my seat belt while he reached into the glove compartment, pulled out a map, and handed it to me. Instantly, I was back in Wisconsin riding in my parents' car.

"Which way do we turn, Ma?" Dad asked.

"Take a left on Route 7," she replied.

"But we want to go north. Are you sure Route 7 goes north?"

"Yah."

But Dad drove past Route 7, then turned at the next road that aimed north. Soon, we were lost. Dad pulled into a gas station.

"Go in and ask directions," he ordered Mom. Mom obediently left the car, with a grim expression on her face. We kids fell silent in the back seat.

"Take a right at the next stop sign and then go left on County P, is what they said," Mom said.

Dad's face screwed up, anger rising, "That can't be right!"

We drove along, taking a right at the stop sign and going left on County P, but something wasn't right. Dad blew up.

"Why can't you get it right? What's wrong with you? Can't you even get simple directions straight?"

Mom flushed. "I gave you directions and you refused to follow them. Next time, go ask yourself."

"Damn it!" he exclaimed. Silent tears of fear crept down my face. I leaned hard against my sister, as if I could hide under her and miss the physical altercation that was about to begin.

Rich's voice interrupted my flashback.

"What do you think is the best way to get to the mall?" he asked.

I was choked up. I pointed to the mall on the map. Then, we bent our heads over the maze of streets and figured it out.

❧ ❧ ❧

After registering and getting my school ID, I found my way to the pool. Each lap removed a layer of anxiety. Odd roommate? It'll be okay; I won't be there that much. Too much new information? It won't be long and it won't feel new. The water slid over my skin and through my brain, sweeping out the complex streets of Atlanta, the cost of the books that my scholarship didn't cover, and my need to get a job to pay the rent.

Hair still wet from the pool, I slipped into the meeting room as the evening orientation session started. My leg muscles bulged under my cutoff shorts. I found a place on the floor with the other students. Most were straight out of college like me.

The first speaker droned on. What the point was, I couldn't begin to remember. The next speaker stood up. He was a second-year student and was he handsome! They introduced him as Ted Smith.

I was so pleased to have a change of pace I called out, "Yeah, Ted!"

"When I first came to Atlanta," he began. I wasn't listening very carefully. I was looking at his knee-high moccasins—too cool!

"I had never lived so far away from the water. I'm from Tidewater, Virginia," he continued. My mind heard the basic facts of how he adjusted to living in Atlanta, but my adrenaline raced ahead. This slim guy with a full beard and soft tenor voice had swept me away.

"You are invited to share in the refreshments, and get to know one another," the host of the evening announced. Everyone stood up and began talking at once. I moved to the refreshment table; swimming had made me hungry. There was Ted. As I filled my small plate, he spoke.

"Hello!" His voice was warm and his brown eyes danced.

"Hi." I felt shy now that we were face to face.

"Where're you from?" he asked.

"Wisconsin," I replied, blushing deeply.

"That's quite a ways away." He smiled an incredible smile. The smile was set off by his satiny brown skin.

"Have you had a chance to see the campus yet?" he asked with kindness and enthusiasm.

"No," I admitted.

"Would you like a personal tour?" There was a soft southern sound in his vowels.

"Ah, okay." I wanted to go. I didn't want to go.

"Shall we go?" he asked. I dropped my bag with its car keys and wet bathing suit in the corner. How far would we go anyway? It was already getting dark.

Walking out of the brick courtyard, we went up the street to the student union. As we talked, my infatuation soared. He was one of six children; so was I! He was a middle child; so was I. The evening seemed to make everything cozy and safe. I relaxed a little in the darkness.

Getting back to Brooks Commons I was shocked to see it was empty. What time was it? Had they locked up? How would I get to my car keys? Panic grew in my mind, but I didn't allow it a voice. The person arrived at the doors to lock up just as we walked up. Picking up my red bag I walked next to dream man down to my car, and we said our goodbyes.

In the morning I hurried from the parking deck up the long hill. The huge auditorium where I went to attend Christian Theology 101 filled quickly. Professor Bill Mallard pushed up his sleeves, put his watch on the outside of his sleeve, and adjusted his black-rimmed, army-issue glasses. His hair stuck out at the sides like Donald Duck's Uncle Scrooge on TV.

Then he began to speak. Energy and passion filled his voice as he drew a little stick figure with a hat and winged feet, which appeared on the overhead projector screen. He began to speak of stories and drew a line across the top of the page and wrote, "God's Story." On a parallel line below the little man, he wrote, "Our Story." Mallard turned and searched the room, drawing us in with his magic and enthusiasm.

"This is Hermes, the Greek god!" he announced with a gigantic smile as if he were announcing the Queen of England. He laughed contagiously. "Well, it's supposed to be Hermes, the Greek god!" He laughed again, even more merrily. "He is the messenger."

He drew an uphill path from Our Story to God's Story, with the winged feet of Hermes on the diagonal line. "Each time we read the Bible we find points where Our Story connects with God's Story," he said. "This course is about Christian Theology. How does the story of the Church connect with God's Story, make sense of it?"

With homework in hand, I made my way from the auditorium out into the sunshine for lunch. The guys were sitting, sprawled out across the steps of the commons. Ted was among them. Almost seventy percent of the seminarians were men. I found a place to sit with a couple of classmates and pulled out my peanut butter sandwich.

Then it was off to Supervised Ministry One (SM1). SM1 was the practical application work that had drawn me to Candler. It was directed by Dan, the chaplain of the regional hospital, and by Dr. Roberta Bondi, my advisor at Candler.

"Let's introduce ourselves," Bondi said. Her red dress, pale skin, and slender physique set off her gray hair. The gray looked chic. She couldn't have been much more than my mother's age, forty-something.

Around the circle we went. I was the only Midwesterner in the group! One woman was from Europe; two were from the deep South, you could hear it in their soft drawl. Most of the men in our group of nine were southern as well.

Bondi began, "Over the coming year, you will share with one another your stories of what happens during your hospital visits (verbatims)."

One week rolled into another in SM1. When a verbatim was given, we were to ask questions.

"Why did you do that?" I asked one of the women after she had given a verbatim. My direct questions were like jackknifed trucks on the freeway of those who had been schooled in the indirect approach of the South. There was always an unnatural pause in the group. It was as if my words had to be properly digested, and the students' mouths patted daintily with fine linen before responding to such abrupt speech.

One morning as students surged toward the lecture hall, a guy wearing blue jeans and a white oxford shirt came toward me. When I realized it was Ted, I grinned. Standing there in my white flats and a sundress Barb had made for me, Ted caught up with me.

"Teresa," he said. "Will you go dancing with me on Friday night?"

"Yes," I said, thinking *yes!* "That'd be fun."

"I'll pick you up at ten o'clock here on campus after the Black Student meeting ends." We agreed on the place and he headed off to his next class.

The week sped by. I spent all of my free time in a panic. What does one wear when going dancing in Atlanta? What do I have that I can wear? What is cute and . . .

Friday came. It seemed like God had hung the stars just for me. I parked and headed for the benches behind the finance building. I laid back and watched the stars. There was no sign of Ted. The gorgeous stars filled the black velvet sky. It felt holy, like a sanctuary. It reminded me of lying in the snow bank behind the barn as a youngster, stargazing and talking to God. Time stood still. Periodically, I would wander out in front of the building to see if Ted was waiting somewhere else; but he wasn't. The night was God holding me in the palm of God's hand, whispering secrets to me.

Suddenly, Ted came rushing up. His face was filled with tension and worry.

"I'm sorry! I'm so sorry. I tried to take Eleanor home after the meeting. You remember her, the elderly woman? She couldn't remember where she lived. We kept driving around and around. I kept asking her if anything looked familiar. I was going crazy thinking I'd never get her home and meet you in time. I am so sorry I'm late."

"It's no problem. What time is it anyway?" I asked. While swaying in God's peaceful hand I had lost track of time. Ted was two hours late! He kept apologizing over and over again as we walked to his car.

"Ah, the Green Machine," he said, as if to introduce me to the bright chartreuse-green, 1976 Datsun. While he opened the car door for me, he apologized again.

"Please stop apologizing," I said.

We were zooming around Atlanta's interstate when he pointed out Baby Does. The dance club lit up the night and looked down upon the city of Atlanta. Soon, the music pulled us in.

Hours later, he led me through the tangle of finely dressed people over to the big plate-glass windows overlooking the city. With his six-feet, two-inch frame behind me, his arms around me, and the city below glittering with lights, it was an enchanted moment. Then he kissed me.

"Ready to go?" he asked a few minutes later. I nodded. He drove me to my car. There we sat, exhausted and wide-awake, and talked.

∾∾∾

"It's for you," my roommate, Doris, warbled after answering the phone the next morning. We had gone to church together; then eaten lunch at her tiny Formica kitchen table.

"Hello," said Ted. I could tell he was smiling.

"Hi."

"Have you caught up on your sleep?" he asked.

"I think so," I replied.

"Want to go for a walk at Lullwater park?" he asked. "How about in half an hour?"

We drove off with the windows wide open to capture the glorious breeze. We held hands and walked. Sitting by the water he talked about his work at the school library. His job was to search out the books that had been shelved incorrectly by a man with dyslexia!

Throughout the next week, the anxiety of being in a new place ate at me. Suffering from bouts of crippling cramps and diarrhea, I found my way to the health center.

"What seems to be the problem?" the woman doctor asked in a clipped sharp manner.

"I'm having cramps here," I placed my hand over my lower abdomen. "Then I get terrible diarrhea."

She palpated my abdomen and questioned me. "How long have you been a student here? Where's home for you?"

After hearing my answers, she announced her conclusion. "You have colonitis. It's caused by stress. Eat fiber. Make sure and exercise." She turned and left the room before I had a chance to say anything.

I went home and had raisin bran for breakfast. Each day after class I would run about a mile, then walk another mile. The colonitis subsided

I was incredulous and Ted seemed oblivious.

"You call every day!" I exclaimed. "This seems pretty serious to me."

"We're having a casual relationship," he would explain. "I call my good friends often."

I tried to back away from Ted's intensity.

A few days later I was at Ted's apartment. We were in the kitchen and he was mumbling under his breath, "It's Jack's turn to clean up the kitchen; but has he done it? No."

I sat at the kitchen table, fixated by the sight of a guy doing the dishes. It was a foreign concept to me. He turned and held up half of a cutting board. "Well, that's that."

"What happened?" I asked.

Ted shrugged. "It broke." He dropped it into the wastebasket.

My mind raced. Something was broken and it was no big deal? No one was in trouble? It was just an everyday thing and you went on with life?

In my mind's eye, I could see spilt milk flooding the supper table. Dad would grab his newspaper and pull it out of the way, barking, "Slop head!!"

"Aren't you going to tell Jack about it?" I asked anxiously. Wouldn't he be angry?

"When I see him, I'll mention it. I guess," Ted remarked, calm as a cucumber lounging in the refrigerator.

"Are you going to buy him a new one?" I pushed.

"No," Ted answered. The broken cutting board swirled in my mind a long time—the idea that something could be broken and be no big deal. It was just something that happened, an accident. What a concept!

Quarterly reviews came up in SM1.

"Please share with each other the gifts and growth you have seen in one another," Professor Bondi said. The idea of people talking about me made me nervous. Surely, they could see I wasn't as intelligent as they were. I didn't fit in at graduate school. The men spoke first. It seemed like it might be okay.

Then Maxine, petite with a pink pedicure, said, "Teresa, why don't you like us?" I was dismayed by her uncharacteristic directness. I flushed a deep red, my mouth hung open but nothing came out.

Bondi ignored the question and gently spoke up, "What other positive growth have you seen in one another?"

The group moved on to share what they saw in one another, but I was stuck. What was the point of saying to Maxine, "I believe your indirect communication is manipulative? Now that the chasm had been pointed out, what would happen next? I dreaded confrontation and its aftermath of violence.

ȣȣȣ

The argument began simply enough. We were sitting in Ted's room. He was on the bed. I was on the floor stretching my legs. Ted started talking about Ernestine. Ernestine was a willowy woman with dark sensuous skin, and athletic to boot. Ted had told me she played tennis with him and they went jogging sometimes. Now he was saying he had dated her some, at the same time he was dating me; but he had chosen me instead of her. I was not happy. Why hadn't he been upfront at the time?

I picked up one of his size fifteen shoes and threw it at him. Not hard, but not a toss either. Then I picked up the next shoe and threw it. Shoe after shoe after shoe ... He protested and caught the shoes. Then he dropped to the floor beside me. He tried to wrap his arms around me. I moved away. He sat still.

"I don't want us to interact this way," he said softly. "I want us to agree that we won't throw things at each other or try to physically hurt each other."

Tears filled my eyes. He moved closer and wrapped his arms gently around me. This man was a gift.

"Hey, what's going on?" he asked, wiping the tears from my cheeks.

"My dad," I began with my voice trembling. "My dad abuses my mom. He hits her ... throws things at her. And she stays. She doesn't leave him." Ted held me quietly. He helped me up and we curled up together. Then he shared with me the memory of his dad hitting his mom.

His mom had called out to the oldest child, "Get me the frying pan." She had knocked his dad out, then divorced him.

SLAYING THE MONSTER

- Teresa's past influences the present. Name some of the ways this happens.
- What helps her through these situations?
- What old ways of doing things does Teresa now see differently?
- What old ways of doing things do you now see differently?

MORE: HEALTHY RELATIONSHIPS

Healing and Hope are Gifts from God. Hope comes from learning that there are other ways to live than being immersed in violence or abuse. Hope can be seen in other people's healthy relationships. Healing comes when we form boundaries based on the knowledge that we are loved by God. God desires for us to live in relationships based on love, respecting ourselves and others as people of value. We are called to value people over things. We are called to respect and love others and ourselves.

To Form Healthy Boundaries, choose a quiet time. Share your love, and your desire for the relationship with the person you love. Talk about God's call to love, then commit yourself to this kind of love. Discuss how you will handle it if one of you becomes disrespectful. Will you call a timeout, and talk it out when you are calm? Will you call on a pastor or counselor?

Hope Grows when we experience healthy relationships and feel God's love for us. Hope grows when we join a Bible Study to better understand God's desire for us. Hope grows when we leave damaging situations and allow other people to help us.

Healing Happens when we tell our story repeatedly and are validated. Healing happens when we continually hand the hurt over to God, forgive ourselves, seek help via friends, family, support groups, spiritual direction, and/or counseling. If you get stuck seek out a professional to help you work through it.

Assurance: God chooses us to be God's people (Genesis 17:7, John 3:16). Jesus forgives us and sends us forth to holy living (John 8:11). We are not supposed to be able to make sense of everything now, but we are to hold hope, love and faith as key to healing (1 Corinthians 13).

6

Intersections and Decisions

GRANDMA SWEET AND I sent each other letters.

Dear Sweetiepie,

How are you? I'm in Florida for the winter with my sister. I've been picking up shells on the beach. Then in the afternoon we get together to play rummy. Florida is a fine place but the humidity is a little much.:) How's school? I've been thinking of you!

Love,
Gramma

I wrote back:

Dear Grandma,

How are you? I'm doing fine. School is great. I love the professors who teach Christian History. This semester I'm taking a Pastoral Care Class. It's not as exciting as the CT class, but it has some good stuff in it.

Remember how I told you I'd met this handsome guy named Ted? I don't think I described what he looked like in my previous letter. He's about six foot, two inches. Grandpa was tall, was he that tall? Ted has dark hair and a beard. His skin is a beautiful brown color. Oh my, I have to get to class. More later.

Love you,
Teresa

She wrote back to me, *Teresa, this is not good. Please find someone else to date.*

I wrote back to her, *Ted is kind, and would never hit me or hurt me. Why does it matter that his skin is brown?*

My mom wrote me a letter, *Grandma is so upset she went to the pastor to talk to him about you dating a man who is not white. She's been praying that God will change your mind.*

I was crushed. My grandma was rejecting a person on skin color! Was racism the fear of the unknown? Is that how you define racism? How could this be? My Grandma was disapproving of my choice? If you had stabbed me, it couldn't have hurt any worse.

As Thanksgiving drew near, Ted and I talked about Christmastime. "Hey, would you like to come to Virginia with me for Christmas?" he asked. I mulled it over. No. That was too serious in relationship terms. Yes. I wanted to see the Atlantic Ocean.

"Okay," I said tentatively, then, "If I drive us to Virginia, then I'll head to Wisconsin for New Year's. Do you want to come home with me?"

"That'd be great. I've never been to the Midwest," Ted answered with enthusiasm.

We stayed at Ted's sister, Rose's house.

"Hello! I've been waiting to meet you," Rose said as she rushed toward me and greeted me with a huge smile. What a great person Rose was; I really enjoyed her.

That night Ted took me to his favorite place: Virginia Beach. I had never been to the ocean. On the way, we passed the ships lit up with white Christmas lights pulled up at the docks. The light glistened off the water, like stars.

At the beach I saw the lifeguard chair and said, "Let's climb up there!" Froth rose in the air. Moonlight filled the sky. I was absolutely mesmerized. "Let's stay here a long time," I said.

All too soon, Ted said, "We need to go; it's way too cold out here."

Soon we were on our way to Wisconsin. Zipping up one interstate and zooming west on another we drove the twenty hours nearly straight through. Arriving bleary eyed, I slept the sleep of the dead the first night home.

The next night, in poured the family. They had waited for me to come home to celebrate Christmas. My married sisters hustled in with homemade pies, dressing, and fruit salad. My teenaged brothers tried to act nonchalant. Finally, it was time to open the presents. The preschool aged grandchildren rushed around the room handing them out. The sound of ripping wrapping paper filled the room.

In the midst of unwrapping things, my dad exclaimed, "Hey, what's this?" and threw his opened present directly at Mom. He was smiling. It was a vice grips! The heavy steel handle slid through the air before we could draw a breath. The blunt-edged vice grips was flying head first over the kitchen table. No one spoke.

Mom looked startled. Putting up one hand, she managed to fend it off, so it didn't hit her in the face or head. There was silence until my little niece asked for something to drink.

At bedtime, Ted and I went upstairs. I sat down on the guest bed next to him.

"Why does he keep doing this? What's wrong with him?" I wept in anguish for my mother, while I cried out in anger with my father. Ted held me and cried with me.

∾ ∾ ∾

"Hello! We're here," I called out as we entered Grandma Sweet's front door.

She came to the door smiling, and hugged me, "Hello, Sweetiepie!" Then, she stood back. I introduced her to Ted.

"Grandma, this is Ted Smith. Ted, this is my grandma." She drew back a little more. Her easy conversation style vanished. We stayed a little while, but there was no conversation to be had. The warmth of my relationship with Grandma had turned bitterly cold.

"Well, we have to be going, I'll see you later." I hugged her and kissed her. We drove back to my folks' house.

Driving back to Atlanta, I cried for miles and miles.

∾ ∾ ∾

"Hey there, Teresa!" Barb called out to me over the phone. "What's new?"

"Hey yourself. I am trying to decide what to do this summer. Second semester is flying by. I don't think I want to stick around for Atlanta's summer heat and humidity. I'm thinking I'll see if I can get a job in the hometown one last time."

"Ohhh. That'd be great to have you here, even for a summer," Barb responded with pleasure. "Have you heard Hans is leaving the church to become a youth director somewhere else?"

"Hmm. No, I didn't know that. What I know is that in two years the bishop will be sending me to serve a church as a pastor and it won't be near our hometown. Plus, I am tired of Ted's 'casual relationship' stuff. Maybe some distance will help him decide if he is serious or not."

"Well, I've got to take off. I have some signs I need to letter for my business," Barb ended the conversation cheerfully.

It wasn't long until I received my home church newsletter and in it was a blurb that said they were searching for a summer intern youth director. It had been weird to have Hans become a youth director in my home church eighteen months ago. I sent in an application to be the summer intern and was hired immediately. Before I knew it, the second semester was over and I was back home for the summer. I met with Hans and quizzed him about the job.

Then I asked, "So which days do you take off?"

"What?" he exclaimed, his big mouth wide open. His face reddened, as he began to bluster, "I thought it would be impossible to kill your work ethic." He went on and on. I was silent. There was no arguing with Hans; he thought he was always right. Just like almost every other man I knew in my hometown.

Seminary had pushed us to be sure we did "self-care;" the word from churches around the country was that pastors were tired and ineffective because they didn't take care of themselves. I could hear the professor in my Pastoral Care Class lecture us:

"If you expect to be able to minister to someone else in the midst of his or her crisis, you must take care of your health. You will need time off to recharge and rest. If you do not take care of yourself: exercising, eating right, taking a day or two off each week, you will not be able to take care of anyone else."

Hans's voice brought me back to the present. I was stony and silent.

I had cut a deal for the summer. To avoid going head to head with Dad daily by living with him and Mom, I was living with my sister, Lisa, and brother-in-law. Instead of paying rent, I was painting their barn for them.

In the evenings long after Lisa had gone to bed, I sat on the back steps under the blanket of stars, stretching the phone cord out the door, talking to Ted.

"Hey, how are you?" he'd ask. Just like that, the night would become brighter.

"Okay," I'd reply. We'd talk about the challenges of his summer job and our plans for the next day.

In June, Ted called and announced, "I'm coming to visit you for the Fourth of July."

"What?" I asked, with excitement and fear.

"Don't you want me to come see you?"

"Yes, but . . ." I didn't know why I felt hesitant. Night after night, we talked.

One ordinary evening he said, "You know, I'm going to ask you to marry me one of these days." It seemed surreal; I couldn't believe it.

"What are you doing this weekend?" I finally asked, immediately wrestling the idea of marriage to the ground and tucking it away in the back of my head.

∽∽∽

July drew near, and I began to fear his arrival. I wanted to tell him not to come. But I couldn't say why. I didn't know why. He flew into Chicago and took the bus to the city nearest to me.

Diesel fumes filled the parking lot; my tall guy got off the bus. What a thrill!

"Hey, Love, how are you?" he asked as he wrapped his arms around me. We chattered away, but before we had driven half an hour, he was asleep with his head resting on my shoulder. Deep in thought, I drove the hour back to the house.

Why was I so jumpy? He said he was going to ask me to marry him, but surely not now. I was glad to have him here, but it just brought back the awful tension with my grandmother. I'd worked hard to ignore it.

Lisa, and her husband, Averill, had gone up north for the weekend, so it was just the two of us in the house. The weekend meandered like kittens playing in the yard. On the Fourth of July there was a buzz in my head, jitteriness in my bones, and uneasiness around the house. I couldn't understand why. Barb kept calling, and asking to talk to Ted. It was weird. She didn't have anything to say to me.

Ted and I headed out to the park for the fireworks. He spread out the blanket. I had barely sat down when he dropped down beside me.

"I love you and I want you to marry me," he said. He took a ring box out of his pocket and placed it in front of me.

I hadn't believed this was coming. What was he thinking? Next month he was leaving for a year in Kenya. I didn't want a long distance engagement.

Searching for words, I blurted out, "How long do I have to answer you?" He didn't answer me. Fireworks burst overhead. Orange showered over blue streaks. Finally, he told me about his day.

Instead of asking my parents for my hand in marriage, he had called to tell them his intentions. He had talked to my mom first. She had asked about kids.

Ted had said, "If we have children, they will be loved."

Mom had said, "I guess we'll know the answer when you come by the house after the fireworks." Then Dad had picked up the phone; Ted had talked to him too. Clearly, they were upset by the idea that I might marry Ted.

If I was uneasy before, now I was on edge. I loved this man. He was the best thing that had ever happened to me. I loved my family. Why couldn't they love him regardless of his skin color? What about all those songs they had taught us in Sunday School? "Red and yellow, black and white … Jesus loves the little children of the world." I had no answer, only a churning stomach and a buzzing headache.

We stopped by my parents' house for their annual Fourth of July get-together. But we only stayed briefly. I was speechless. They were polite.

I tossed and turned all night. Praying hard. In the morning I decided. Yes. I would say, "Yes."

I told Ted, "Yes, I will marry you." He kissed me with great joy. I drove to my parents' house to tell them.

Sitting down at the table next to the pancakes and my Dad, I said, "I am going to marry Ted." The newspaper was spread out across the table in front of Dad and he was eating pancakes. He didn't look up from what he was reading, didn't speak. That wasn't so unusual.

Mom was packing Dad's lunch. Her back was to me as she stood at the kitchen counter cutting cheese and spreading mustard. She kept on packing his lunch. She didn't speak either. The silence stretched out.

"Well, I guess I'll be going. I just wanted you to know first," I said as I left.

Back at Lisa's house, I helped Ted get ready to head back to Atlanta. I was sleep-deprived and weary. Torn. I talked to my sister and told her about my engagement, and that Ted was going to Africa for a year, starting next month. I shared with her my discomfort of having a long distance engagement.

"Maybe he'll go there, and not come back," she remarked, in response to my uncertainty. Everywhere I turned, my family and friends were silent. I decided to make a trip to see Hans. Hans was more worldly, had served in the military. Surely, he knew black people were the same as whites and would support me.

"Hey there," I called out as I entered the front door.

"How are you?" he asked. It was like no time had passed at all. He sat down on the same couch with his great belly and swept his hair over his bald spot. I plopped down in the recliner.

"I'm getting married to Ted Smith. He's this great guy. Everything is super, except my family is upset because he is black."

"Teresa, you don't want to be an Oreo. That's no way to live," Hans declared. I left his house with my heart crushed

That night with a heavy heart, I called Ted.

Screwing up my courage, I spoke, "Ted, I love you very much. But I can't do this. I can't be engaged right now. It's too hard. You aren't even going to be here in the country. I'm not saying no, not ever. I'm saying no, not now." I studied the floorboards next to the rug in the living room while I talked.

He was quiet; then, he said, "If you ever want to marry me, you'll have to ask me." We went on to superficialities before hanging up for the night. We continued to call one another each night. I drove down to Atlanta early so I could spend time with him for a week or two before he flew off to Kenya. The weeks were good, like old times, but the broken engagement had left broken glass on the sidewalks of our lives.

❧❧❧

Ted's last day in country was like a clown car with people pouring in and pouring out, going every which way. Ted placed the last of his things in his suitcase. Suddenly, he straightened up with a horrified look on his face.

"My tuition check! I need to go pick up the check from Candler so I can take it with me. We've got to get it before we go to the airport."

He had already left the Green Machine at his sister's house in Virginia, so I was his transport. We jumped in the car and drove down to campus. The check had been promised weeks ago. First, we rushed to the Administration Building; no, it wasn't there. Then, we hustled over to the Finance Department; it wasn't quite ready.

"You should not take this money with you to Africa. The market is way too volatile to keep it in an account over there," the school official told Ted. "You should have someone keep it in an account here and send it to you as needed." Ted checked his watch. There wasn't much time.

We headed to the bank two blocks away. Even with the air conditioner blowing full tilt, sweat ran down our backs.

"Will you keep it in your account?" Ted asked me.

I pursed my lips and frowned. "I'll do it, but I don't like to mix money with relationships." In my book, money equaled trouble. It reminded me of my parents and their troubles.

"Did you send Weidenhoffer his bill?" Dad asked.

"No, not yet." Mom's body stiffened in response to the question.

"Why not?" Dad demanded, irritation spreading across his face like wildfire.

Mom began to answer, "I spent all day in the field …"

He ignored her response and went on to the next complaint. "Have you sent out the bills for the last two jobs I did?"

"I spent all day in the field," she repeated.

"Where are the estimates I wrote up last night?" he interrupted angrily. "I left them right here on the kitchen table." He slammed his fist on the table. Mom glanced wearily at the kitchen table. Of course, it had been cleared to put supper on the table.

"I don't know why you can't keep track of your things," she remarked sourly as she rushed over to try and locate the missing estimates.

I worked hard to push away the memories and convince myself everything would be okay. Besides, there was no choice; Ted's plane was due to take off this very afternoon. I went to the teller to deposit the money in my account.

"Just a minute," responded the teller. He went off to talk to his supervisor about putting a check from a second party, for such a large amount, in my account. Minutes ticked by slowly. We hardly spoke. What was there to say? He was flying off to be an exchange student for a year in Kenya. I would be here.

Ted stared at the clock. It was less than two hours before his plane would take off. The bank representative was on the phone with Candler.

Finally, the teller counted out the cash Ted would need. Back at the house, Ted madly grabbed his bags and hustled out to the car. We maneuvered through the maze of cement jersey walls; cars were crossing lanes from either side as we crept toward the airport.

"We're cutting it too close!" Ted exclaimed with frustration. There was only one hour remaining before his flight took off. Half an hour later, the car jerked to a halt at the glass doors labeled "International Passengers." He jumped out of the car as I popped the trunk.

As he was pulling his two bags out I twisted around in the driver's seat and said, "I'll see you inside in just a minute." My head swiveled back and forth searching for a parking space, as he dashed inside.

Once parked, I ran to the door. Which way was it to the international gate? There it was! I rushed over. The sign read, "Passengers Only."

Frustration and anger overflowed as I trudged back to the car. I sat watching airplanes take off. Which one was Ted in? *Dear God, watch over him!* I prayed.

Within a week and a half, slender blue airmail letters began to fill my mailbox. Not just one or two, but even three arrived on some days!

My love, I'm sorry we didn't get to say goodbye, read the first one.

No one was at the airport to pick me up, the second one said.

The third letter shared, *We eat the same thing every day. How I miss you, my love.*

At first I wrote letters about hypothetical stuff: *If we do get married, what do you think about kids? Where would we live?* or *What are you really like?* Then as time marched on, I began to write "Dear John" letters. *You are far away. I don't want to take care of your money. I don't know what to say anymore.*

He wrote, *I have to take a bus for more than two hours to get to my church placement. The drivers are crazy. There are these "almost crashes" all the time.*

He wanted me to say, "Ted, I love you. Stay near me in Georgia while I finish my last year of seminary, instead of going back to Virginia."

Fear took hold of me. What-ifs ruled my thoughts. What if he took a church in Georgia because of me and then we broke up? The pressure was too much. I wrote, *Ted, do what is best for you. Go back to Virginia this coming summer and serve a church there …*

His next letter said, *My friends say I should give your dad a cow; then I can marry you.* A cow! He was joking, but it didn't seem funny to me. Trade me for a cow! I thought not.

The first of November arrived with a familiar airmail letter, *I have decided to come back and finish my last semester at Candler.*

Come home early? I wanted to be out of his life, safe from all possible connections. I would not get married. I would not repeat my parents' marriage. No face-to-face contact had eroded my confidence in "us" once and for all.

Dragging my feet, I drove to the airport to pick him up right before Thanksgiving. He came through the double doors from Customs. Thin. Bearded. Brown. Same smile. His voice danced through the weariness of the time changes and jet lag. He smiled his huge irresistible grin. Hugged me. Kissed me. Holding back from him, I drove him to my apartment.

Once inside the door, he murmured into my hair, "I've missed you. I love you." Then, as he gathered me into his arms, he said, "I couldn't wait to see you." He kissed my eyebrows, my cheeks, then, my lips. Pulling back for a moment, he looked deep into my eyes, "Teresa, I really do love you."

Then I started falling in love all over again. At the same time, I tried to avoid connection. Why would anyone love me? How could anyone love me? I couldn't conceive it, let alone believe it. So I pushed him away.

Now I was the one saying, "It's casual. Date whoever you want."

 confirmed confirmed confirmed

I had been working afternoons and nights at a Donut Shop during the fall. Regulars came in during my 11 p.m. to 7 a.m. Friday shift: Isaac, a Jewish guy, at eleven and Brandon, a middle-aged redneck, at midnight. They would stay for their wind-down time and amble out after half an hour or so, leaving behind tremendously generous tips.

When Ted started dropping by and the Donut Shop regulars found out I was dating a black man, they stopped coming by.

December and January moved like a blur. February arrived and the reality that Ted was going to graduate and be gone next year descended upon me. Did I want to be single the rest of my life? I loved this man. There'd never been anyone more supportive of me in my life. Would I ever meet anyone better than Ted Smith, more loving and kind, patient and generous? What did God want me to do? I decided to ask Ted to marry me.

First, I took him to a romantic little restaurant that I liked. The food wasn't what I remembered and gave no pleasure to Ted. I couldn't get the words out of my mouth. I needed a Plan B.

Ice cream. We would go out for a walk and ice cream. We purchased our ice cream and walked slowly through the night. Anxiety choked back the words. Finally we drove back to my apartment.

In the quiet with Ted's arms around me, I got the words out, "Will you marry me?"

Ted paused. Then he said, very seriously, "How long do I have to answer you?"

"What?" I drew away from him.

"How long do I have to answer you?" he repeated the question looking innocent!

Speechless, I pushed him away and sat alone. The seconds seem to stretch out like the line at an amusement park, snaking back and forth, loop after endless loop. I glared.

He reached over to me, laughing, "Yes. Yes, I will marry you." He kissed me. "When? When shall we get married?" I gave him a hard time about waiting to answer me before I got serious about answering his question.

"I want to finish school first," I said. "I think it'd be too hard to get married and try to finish school at the same time. How about after I graduate in May next year?" Ted was so happy; he would have agreed to any date. He was slated to go back to Virginia and take an appointment pastoring a church in June. I began to work on getting a job somewhere near or at least in Virginia for the summer.

∾ ∾ ∾

Candler required every second year student do a Professional Assessment half way through the three-year program. The P.A. entailed preaching a sermon, and writing a long theological paper. The tension in the brick courtyard was deep. Every second-year student was hunkered down. I'd worked on my paper for months. I wrote a sermon and practiced it. Still agonizing over it, I turned the packet in to my advisors, Dr. Fred Craddock and Dr. Roberta Bondi.

In the meantime, I had a test to take for the Wisconsin Conference for my admittance as a probationary member of the Wisconsin Annual Conference of the United Methodist Church. It was the next step in becoming an ordained minister in the UMC. I worked on the written test, reading every word in the *United Methodist Book of Discipline*.

After mailing in the test, I drove to Wisconsin for the interviews. All of the potential probationers met for two days at Camp Asbury for interviews. The second day we were called, one by one, back to the room with the interview team. At the end of the day we were called back into the room individually and given the answer.

"We believe you have the potential to be an excellent pastor. You will be ordained a probationary member of the Wisconsin Annual Conference this May 1987," the committee affirmed me!

I shook my head numbly, "Thank you."

Driving back to Atlanta I thought the whole thing had been too easy. If they'd really known who I was, they'd have said no.

Dr. Bondi called me into her office. She engaged in a little chitchat then paused.

"Are you suicidal?" she asked.

I was stunned, "No."

"I read your theological paper," she continued, "and I'm concerned about you. I'm concerned about the domestic violence in your family. Would you like a continuance for your Professional Assessment?"

I was confused. "No, I'm ready."

The day of the Professional Assessment arrived. I made my way up the stairs to the classroom slowly. I had dressed carefully with hose and heels. Clutching my papers tightly, I knocked on the classroom door. Dr. Craddock opened the door with a welcoming smile. I knew he was rooting for me. Dr. Bondi greeted me too, but her expression was somber.

Standing behind the wobbly lectern, I preached my sermon. I rushed through the words like the building was on fire, trying hard to pause at the appropriate points. My face was as red as a tomato.

"Have a seat, Teresa," Dr Craddock invited me with his finest Southern hospitality. They took turns asking questions and making comments. It wasn't as painful as I thought it would be.

"Teresa, please give us a few moments and we'll call you back in," Dr. Bondi requested kindly.

Less than fifteen minutes later Dr. Craddock stuck his head out the door and said, "Please come in."

After I was seated, they began:

"Your sermon was fine."

"The paper you wrote was thorough."

Dr. Craddock, Candler's Preaching Professor, continued, "Teresa, we're concerned. Every sermon must have hope in it. It must have an element of the resurrection. You are a fine preacher, but you're preaching survival. Your paper reflects this as well. We want you to thrive. We want more for you than to just survive."

Dr. Bondi spoke next, "We are advising you to go for pastoral counseling next year. There is an excellent counselor that I'd recommend," she continued on with the information. I couldn't hear anything, except the sound of my heart drowning in despair.

Me?! I had to go to counseling? There was nothing wrong with me! Humph. Who did they think they were? I'd confessed in my theological paper that I'd wished I were dead in junior high school, but what did that have to do with now?

Advised to go to counseling? Was this mandatory for graduation? I wanted to wiggle out. But I didn't ask any questions. I stewed about it instead.

SLAYING THE MONSTER

- What new awareness did Teresa gain in this chapter?
- How might she have gone about evaluating options and details?
- Why did she choose what she chose?
- Did the choice move her toward health and wholeness? How?
- In pairs, examine a decision you have made and whether it helped you move toward health and wholeness.

MORE: COUNSELING INFORMATION

Counselors usually have a degree in social work and are licensed. Your faith community leader may also do counseling.

Beginning Counseling: The client (you) chooses a counselor. Check the counselor's credentials and specialties. During the first session you tell about yourself to give the counselor insight so he or she can better assist you. The client tells the counselor his or her goal is.

Is it Working? The counselor should tell you whether the goal is achievable, and how he or she will help you achieve it. Bench marks should be established. Schedule regular reviews. If progress isn't occurring review it with your counselor, and if need be, find a new counselor.

Spiritual Directors work with a person monthly to help him or her experience God in new ways. For more information or to find an

S.D. in your area, ask your faith community leader or go to www
.sdiworld.org.

Assurance: God works through counselors to help us grow in wholeness and health. Jesus trained the first S. D.s (his disciples), who then
trained others. Mark 6, 14. Acts. Romans 16.

7

The Way of the World

THE REVEREND EUGENE CARTER, District Superintendent of the Lynchburg District, called. "Ted, we are appointing you to serve three African American churches in Lynch Station."

"Lynch Station! What kind of a place is that for a black man to serve?" Ted exclaimed.

Gene explained, "Lynch is a family name." Now that we knew where Ted was going, I applied to the Hinson Rural Life Center Intern Program in North Carolina. They worked with small churches throughout the Southeast. I made a special request to be placed near Lynchburg, Virginia, if possible. The letter I received read in part:

> Dear Teresa,
>
> Welcome! We have chosen you to be one of our summer interns. We look forward to meeting you at our Hinton Rural Life Center for orientation. The following week, you will go to serve Mount Pisgah U.M.C., and Good Shepherd Church Camp in North Carolina.

With a skip in my step and a grin on my face I went looking for Ted on campus. I ran into him on his way to class.

"Guess what?" I whispered, beaming.

"What?" he asked.

"Hinton hired me as a summer intern! I'll be less than two hours away from you."

He grinned, "Hey! That's great."

Ted's graduation came and went. Before I knew it, we were standing next to the beloved Green Machine in the parking lot. After a long hug and stretched out good-byes, I shut the door firmly and leaned in through the open window for one last kiss.

"Have a safe drive! I'll see you in a few weeks."

The future was ours we thought. Little did we know what lay ahead.

〜〜〜

Having passed the test and interview I arrived at the Wisconsin Annual Conference in May ready to be ordained a Deacon. I strode up to the platform in my borrowed black robe. Grandma Sweet, Barb and Mom were glowing, seated next to Pastor Lu and Ted. Receiving the blessing, charge, and ordination of the Deacon was like watching something happen to someone else on a film. Unbelievable.

Ted and I made an appointment to talk to the bishop of Wisconsin about the future.

"We are in need of gifted black pastors," the bishop said sincerely.

"How many black pastors are there in the Wisconsin Conference?" Ted asked.

"Less than five," the bishop continued. "We have strict guidelines in terms of the appointment of minorities. We do not send minority pastors to serve in the northern areas of Wisconsin. It is simply too dangerous, too much racism."

"Tell us about how you handle clergy couples," I queried.

"Clergy couples are great. I don't have to think about someone's request to keep their wife near a hospital because she's a nurse, or whatever. I can work with both pieces of the puzzle. The understanding in Wisconsin is that God comes first. Therefore, we do not promise clergy couples that they will be able to live together. We do have a policy that they will be appointed no more than 200 miles apart. We make exceptions for newlyweds in their first appointment, but after that we follow the regular policy."

Living up to two hundred miles apart? I wasn't willing to do that if I could help it.

Less than a week later I landed in the foothills of western North Carolina. Hinton Rural Life Center, a mission post of the United Methodist Church, was designed to build up the small churches of the South. Meeting me at the parking lot were long rows of vegetables.

After a few days orientation, I headed east toward the Piedmont area. By early evening, I had made it to the church camp. I was given a warm welcome, shown the bunkhouse, and left to rest well. It was echoingly empty. I tossed and turned, then called Ted on the office phone, collect.

"Hey, Baby," I said in a low voice, as if I might disturb the bats outside on their mosquito-eating mission.

"Hey, you," came the warm reply.

"I'm here now, at the camp."

"That's good."

I could hear that Ted was sunk into a sofa. I leaned forward in my chair as if I could get closer to him that way. "What's new?"

He spoke with a longing in his voice, "I miss you. This three-bedroom house is huge. Wait until you see it." He had moved into his parsonage the week before. "I spent today trying to see the people who are sick. Some of their driveways are so rough, I'm afraid to drive the car down them. I've been walking the quarter mile from the road to their houses.

"Let me tell you, figuring out where each person lives is the biggest challenge of all! One of the key leaders in the church, Bethene, told me to come past the old store and turn by Dick's to get to her house. I had to ask her where Dick's was. She told me to turn left at the old tree on the corner."

He laughed. I felt warmed by his laughter all the way through the telephone line.

"I'll come up and see you in a couple days!" I said eagerly.

"Bethene said you can stay with her when you come to visit." Propriety demanded that a single woman not stay at the single preacher man's house, engaged or not.

Throughout the summer, we got together at Lynch Station, or Mt. Pisgah as time allowed. We continued to research what to do next year.

"I've always wanted to serve a church in Wisconsin," I told Ted earnestly. "I love the snow and they have given me money for seminary, so I'd like to pay them back, although the money was given with no strings attached."

"Virginia is the only place to live," he countered. "It has mountains and beaches, as well as big cities. There are more than a thousand churches in Virginia, so it's a big pond as United Methodist Conferences go," Ted spoke with passion and love.

"The Wisconsin Annual Conference has two hundred and fifty appointments they can send clergy to serve," I said. "It's what? One-fourth the size of Virginia? I understand that. You're right, Virginia is a nice place; but more than that we actually have seminary friends in Virginia. That's important," I said. "Then there's the issue of prejudice, in Wisconsin it seems people will be kind to your face and then stab you in the back. They can't seem to be truthful about being racist. That's Northern racism.

In the South, if people are racist they tell you to your face. I certainly prefer honesty and folks who are up-front."

Ted reflected on his financial situation. "The other thing is that I owe the Virginia Conference. They don't give grants like the Wisconsin Conference. You have to repay the money you used for school, with years of service as a pastor in Virginia," Ted said.

We were sitting on the front porch steps of his house swatting at the mosquitoes. The parsonage didn't have air conditioning, so it was "cooler" outside, where at least the air moved when a car drove by. I eyed the red dirt in the yard with ongoing fascination. I had never known red dirt. How could red dirt grow a thing?

"Wouldn't it be great if we could live a few years in each place and then decide?" I said dreamily, with my back against his knees. Then with a more sober voice, "I don't want to get sucked back into my family's unhealthy stuff. Could I go back to Wisconsin and be strong enough not to succumb to it?"

"If we are going to stay in Virginia we ought to meet with some of the district superintendents, and the bishop of Virginia this summer," Ted said, ever the planner.

"Okay. You set up the times, and places; I will be there," I agreed.

∾∾∾

The little church I was interning at was predominantly elderly and all white. One day, race relations came up.

"It says in the Bible that races aren't supposed to intermingle," one older lady said with certainty.

"That's what God tells Moses in Exodus; don't let the people marry people of other towns," her next door neighbor agreed, as she set the flowers on the altar. No one knew I was engaged to a black man. They assumed that "people of other towns" meant people of other races.

"It's like birds. God made them all, but cardinals and sparrows don't mate," a seventy-year-old man stated. No one seemed to know that after the death of his first wife, Moses married a Cushite woman, an African. My heart was filled with pain. How could they believe it was wrong to love someone?

∾∾∾

Ted and I traveled to Charlottesville to visit our friends Jane and Ryan.

"Congratulations on your engagement!" Jane said as she hugged me.

"You need to go meet with our district superintendent; he's a good guy," Ryan enthused. "Wouldn't it be great if you guys were appointed to serve churches near us?" We made an appointment with Ryan's superintendent.

"Hello, Ted and Teresa," the superintendent shook our hands with enthusiasm. "I'm glad you could come by. Ryan told me about the two of you." He was thoughtful. "I think there are strong possibilities here in the district. If the two of you need appointments next year, I will find churches for you to serve," he spoke with assurance.

We left his office beaming. Maybe this whole appointment thing would come together. After all, people kept telling us Virginia was short of clergy, and a bigger shortage of pastors was coming soon.

Ted had scheduled an appointment with his bishop. The bishop's secretary met us and said, "It will be just a moment." Moments later we followed her into the bishop's office.

The bishop stood and shook our hands without emotion, "Ted. Teresa." The bishop leaned back in his desk chair as Ted began to speak.

"Bishop, we are going to be married in May next year. We would like to arrange for Teresa to serve a church in Virginia."

"Ted," the Bishop answered, still leaning back in his chair. "I'll tell you, clergy couples are difficult. They are troublesome. You know, this is my last year before I retire. I don't want to leave any problems for the next bishop." He closed his eyes momentarily, then slowly opened them, part way.

"Bishop," I asked, "How many clergy couples are there in Virginia?"

"Thirty-five, or so," he responded. "It's very difficult to appoint them to churches that are geographically near to each other. That's a lot of couples to work with and it's not helpful at all."

I tried to sound patient and thoughtful, "Bishop, I'm not sure I understand. I am from the Wisconsin Conference, and they have close to forty clergy couples. Their conference is about one-fourth the size of Virginia. The Wisconsin bishop sees clergy couples as an advantage in the appointment process."

The bishop leaned back further in his chair, and gazed at the ceiling. Slipping his shoes off, he rubbed his stocking feet together.

"Teresa, why don't you just go home and darn socks?" the bishop asked. With that, our time with the bishop was over.

Back in Atlanta for my third year, I received a letter in the mail. Gripping its white linen in my hand, I tried to find a quiet place to read. Not an easy thing to do with camp kids milling around, moving from Bible study, to crafts, to swim time. The return address read "Richmond, Virginia." The official letter read:

> *Dear Teresa,*
> *It is with regret I write to inform you that at the present time we do not have an appointment to offer you in the Virginia Annual Conference.*

Even before I dialed the phone, the tears were running down my cheeks. I brushed them angrily away.

"Hey, my love," Ted said, when he answered the phone.

"The bishop sent me a letter stating he has no appointment for me, and I haven't even officially asked for one," I exclaimed. We strategized how to approach his bishop in Virginia again. Because we had not officially requested an appointment for me in Virginia, his letter was out of order. We needed to go through the whole process officially, in order.

"Before we do anything else with my bishop, you need to contact your bishop in Wisconsin." Ted explained.

Sitting cross-legged on the carpeting in my Atlanta apartment, I asked Ted over the phone, "What for?"

"You need to ask for permission to serve a church in the Virginia conference, before we officially ask the bishop of Virginia for an appointment for you. Check out the paragraph in the *Book of Discipline* first," Ted reminded me.

With deep sighs I hung up the phone. I dragged myself to the desk and wrote to the bishop in Wisconsin:

> *September 10, 1987*
>
> *Dear Bishop,*
>
> *I appreciate the time you spent with Ted and me. Given our current circumstances, I request that I be allowed to serve under appointment in the Virginia Annual Conference per paragraph 421. The United Methodist Book of Discipline 1984 for the 1988–1989 appointment year.*
>
> > *Sincerely,*
> > *Teresa*

After licking the envelope and frowning at the taste, I chugged down some water. Next letter up: the Virginia Bishop's copy of the Wisconsin letter. I felt hopeless dropping them into the mailbox on the way to school the next day.

The sunshine in the seminary courtyard didn't feel as friendly with Ted in Virginia. I sat and stewed about what I had to do next: call the counseling service like Dr. Bondi and Dr. Craddock had told me to do.

Finally, I made the call and set up the appointment. The prefab building squatted under the pines. The receptionist greeted me nicely enough. Before I even had the chance to steel myself for what was to come, the counselor was beckoning me.

"You must be Teresa," he said, and extended his hand in welcome. I smiled politely and murmured.

"Have a seat," his middle-aged face seemed sincere enough.

"Tell me about yourself." The invitation sounded like a command to me.

Shakily, I began, "I grew up on a farm in Wisconsin, the third child of six, middle of the girls. My parents . . ." I cleared my dry throat, "my parents . . . I guess you would call it domestic violence."

He asked for details and I reluctantly gave them.

When the hour ended, he said, "I grew up on a farm in Wisconsin too. This seems to be a common theme for farm children. It happened to me when I was growing up."

I went straight home and lay down. Groaning and moaning, I prayed, *God, how could you send me to meet with this man? Isn't it enough that I am in pain? I have to meet other people who are in pain! Who says it is a condition of farm families? I can't stand it,* I cried. *Do I have to go back?*

I felt as if my intestines had been pulled out foot by foot and showed to this guy and he glanced and said, "Hmm, just like mine" in a cavalier way.

Go back I did, but not to that man. Thankfully, he was far too expensive. I began to meet with a student counselor. The man seemed old, at least thirty-something.

My counselor, Steve, asked, "What do you want to work on?" I was ready for the question.

"I want to make certain that my upcoming marriage will not be like my parents' marriage," I announced. Week after week, I went in and shared. I felt unloved by my dad.

The counselor said, "What do you want him to say and do? You take this chair and pretend you are him. Say what you need him to say." Steve was helpful and I was glad to be doing something proactive about my upcoming marriage. The door to the future beckoned us.

It wasn't long before the Virginia superintendent who was Chair of the Cabinet of Superintendents called Ted.

"Ted, we have an appointment for Teresa. We'll combine the four black churches up by Bedford with your three black churches down by Lynch Station. You will be the senior pastor and she can be the associate pastor," he said it with great satisfaction, having solved a difficult conundrum.

"I'll talk to Teresa and get back to you," Ted's anger rose and his frustration spiked. He jabbed the phone digits as he dialed Atlanta.

"Hello!"

"Hey," Ted spoke ominously. I slumped to the floor, trying to steel myself against the news that was to come.

"You won't believe it," he began in a rush of words. After telling all about the call, he asked, "Can you believe the audacity?"

I rubbed hard at a scuff mark on the kitchen floor, as if I could rub out the ridiculousness of the situation, then burst out saying, "That's not fair to the churches! It's an impossible distance for us to be effective as their pastors. I bet they were never even consulted. They're creating an impossible situation. It's more than two hours between the northernmost church and southernmost church." Ted glumly agreed.

"We've always said we don't want the stress of working together at the same church," I thought out loud. "The last thing I want to do is work with and be married to the same person."

Back in Virginia, the bishop was untiring in his letter writing. Opening the mailbox I found an electric bill and a letter. Hmm. Uhhhh, it had the official bishop insignia on it. Kicking open the apartment door, I put away the groceries like I was a robot. The letter stared at me from the counter. Cradling the phone receiver between my head and shoulder, I dialed Ted's number.

"Ring. Ring. Ring." No answer. I lay down on my unmade bed, tore open the letter, and began to read.

Dear Teresa,

We regret to inform you that the Virginia Annual Conference does not have an appointment for you.

In essence it said: We offered you an appointment. You refused. We are no longer obligated, because you turned down what we offered. We have no appointment for you. There really wasn't any time to dwell on it. I stalked out to the car with a backpack full of homework and headed toward the suburb of Buckhead, where I watched two children for a couple every Monday night. Aiming my grungy Escort down the streets lined with fairytale homes, I finally parked at the curb and went up to the house where I would watch the children.

By the time the parents came home my car clock read "11:00." At home, I paced back and forth while I dialed Ted's number.

After a lengthy conversation, we agreed Ted should contact the Wisconsin bishop; it didn't look like the Virginia bishop was going to offer me anything else.

The next day Ted called and set up an appointment to see the Wisconsin bishop.

Then he began to call his friends, "Hey, I need to let you know I'm leaving Virginia to serve in Wisconsin."

The responses to the bishop's decision not to offer me another position were immediate and startled:

"What?!"

"That isn't right."

"This isn't fair."

"It's against the *Discipline.*"

"Definitely discrimination."

A group of thirty friends—men and women, black and white, young and old and in between—came together to strategize how to keep Ted in Virginia and get an appointment for me too.

They shared ideas, then concluded they should each contact their own superintendents and ask him or her if an appointment could be found for Ted and Teresa. They agreed on the strategy. One by one, they contacted each and every one of the eighteen Virginia superintendents for conversation and clarity.

"To deny someone an appointment who is a woman when we are saying there is a clergy shortage is nothing short of sexism."

"To allow Ted to leave the Virginia Conference when we need strong black clergy is a travesty."

"To refuse to give someone an appointment simply because they are a part of a clergy couple is discrimination. If it isn't put right, we'll be contacting the watchdog agencies of the church: The Committee on Religion and Race, The Committee on the Status and Role of Women."

With high hopes, we let go of the idea of Wisconsin appointments and decided to cast our lot with Virginia. All was quiet for a while. Winter folded into spring.

It was all about my future, my life; but I wasn't included. The second-hand account went something like this. Ted sat working on his worship plans when the phone rang.

"Hello, Ted, this is the bishop calling. I am sitting in the cabinet meeting here in Richmond, and wanted to discuss Teresa's appointment prospects with you."

"Hello, bishop," Ted answered, trying to be cordial.

"We are on speaker phone here; I've just asked the cabinet whether they have an appointment for Teresa. There is none."

"Bishop, I'm getting in my car right now. I will be there as soon as possible. I want to look in the eyes of the cabinet members as they tell me there is no appointment. Several of them have given me their word they would provide a place for Teresa; and I want to hear from them for myself."

"Ted, there is no reason for you to come here today. This is a closed session, not open to clergy or others," the bishop spoke strongly.

"Bishop, you may make it so that I have to leave the Virginia Conference, but one day I will be back to walk on your grave." The conversation ended.

Scarcely had the phone receiver been put down when the senior African American superintendent called Ted.

"Ted, take a deep breath now. Settle down. The bishop thinks you are threatening to kill him. Whatever you do, *do not* come to Richmond."

Ted relayed the rest of the conversation to me with great anger and disgust. I received the sorry news with a heart of stone.

Ted's gravelly voice was choked. He had been loyal to Virginia and this was his reward. No one on the cabinet seemed willing to stand up to the bishop; it wasn't a matter of whether there were churches available for me to serve. It was a matter of the bishop's decision.

Ted's next call to Wisconsin revealed they had no vacancies. One last letter made its way forlornly to the Virginia Bishop. This one stated:

> Bishop,
>
> While I understand the Virginia Conference makes it a high priority to appoint clergy couples in proximity to each other, I am strongly called by God to serve as a pastor in the local church. Therefore, I request that I be given an appointment without thought of proximity to Ted. I will serve anywhere I am appointed in the Virginia Conference.
>
> Sincerely,
> Teresa

One last letter made its way to Atlanta from Virginia.

> Teresa,
> There is no appointment for you in the Virginia Conference.

So it was in April that I sent my last letter to the bishop in Wisconsin in order to follow the rules of the *Book of Discipline*.

> Dear Bishop,
> I write to request that I be given a Voluntary Leave of Absence. At this time, the Bishop of the Virginia Annual Conference has informed me no appointment can be found in the Virginia Conference for me. Therefore, I will seek employment in other ministry settings apart from serving a local church.

My heart was not just heavy; it was sunk in a sea of sorrow. I had spent three long years working to follow God's will. Now I would not be given a church to serve.

Graduation was joyful, but rather empty. Red roses filled my arms and my smile was recorded for posterity; but the future seemed without purpose. Heading back to my apartment with my roommate, Karen, Ted and I and our friends crowded in to celebrate the day and pack things up. Spending a quiet moment in my bedroom, the grief of it all caught me. In my hands lay my diploma. In my heart lay cement blocks. The phone rang; I dully answered it.

"Teresa?" the unfamiliar male voice inquired.

"Yes, this is she."

"Teresa, this is the Chair of the Cabinet, and Superintendent of the Roanoke District. I'm calling on behalf of the Virginia Annual Conference. We have an appointment for you, if you are interested."

"Yes," I replied, smoothing my graduation dress, not trusting myself to say more. I grabbed my journal and opened the bedside drawer to get a pen.

"Teresa, we are offering you the Eagle Rock Charge on the Roanoke District. It's not too far from Ted's churches. There are four small churches that comprise the Charge. Will you accept this appointment?"

My mouth hung open. With a whirlwind of thoughts, I said, "Yes."

"Fine, Teresa, fine," the superintendent responded. "I look forward to meeting you at the Virginia Annual Conference next month which will be held in Roanoke."

The phone dangled there as I scrawled out the words, "Eagle Rock Charge, four churches: Bethel, Shiloh, Glen Wilton, and Eagle Rock, Roanoke District." The incessant beeping of the phone reminded me I had not hung up the receiver. The laughter from the other room pulled me back to reality.

I flew down the hall and burst into the living room: "I've got an appointment in Virginia!" I felt as if I had been snatched from an empty, purposeless existence. All was not in vain. God was faithful.

A pounding feeling woke me up the next day. What was it? It was my own heart responding to the impending uncertainty and responsibility, the awesome weight of being a pastor to not just one church, but four churches!

SLAYING THE MONSTER

- Examine the process that took place between Ted and his friends.
- Can you determine what caused others to "*See*" the dilemma?
- What action was taken to "*Learn*" more about it and strategize?
- What follow-through "*Act*" took place to address the dilemma?
- When have you experienced bias? What happened?

MORE: RACISM, SEXISM, AND JUSTICE INFORMATION

Racism and Sexism are facts of life. Even when we think we have left prejudice and bias behind, it sneaks along into the future with us, hiding in the crevices of our shoes, lingering in our institutions, and lying under the rugs in our churches. Each of us has prejudices.

Sometimes we see them and are aware of them; sometimes we are blind because it "has always been that way."

Justice occurs when three things happen. First, the person who has experienced the prejudice tells other people about it with sincerity and integrity. Second, other people who have experienced the same kind of prejudice share their experiences, and we learn we are not alone. Third, a group of people who have lived through it, and their supporters, gather together in solidarity and decide to speak out. Each step is more difficult. Justice requires endurance.

Assurance: God calls us to do justice (Amos 5:24). God loves justice (Psalms 9, 13).

8

Four Churches and a Mountain

"LET'S GO! LET'S GO!" we urged each other on. We were going to do the "preacher drive-by." Having packed up and left Atlanta following my graduation, we were now at Ted's parsonage. My sister, Barb, and her friend had been studying the map with me. Where were the four churches located? The superintendent had said they weren't very far from Ted's churches.

Dusk was falling as we analyzed the roads between Lynch Station and Eagle Rock, Virginia. There was no straight line. The Blue Ridge Mountains rose up between the two.

Piling into the car, Ted took the wheel and sent us spinning down a crooked highway. Thirty minutes later, we had yet to cross the mountain ridge. Ascending the hairpin turns, we saw the shadow of the Peaks of Otter in the gloaming. Upon arriving at the top of the mountain, we took one quick left turn and then one short right turn. Hardly a minute passed before we were headed down the mountain, hairpin turn by hairpin turn.

At the base of the mountain lay the streetlights of Buchanan; the lights looked weary of pushing to illuminate the town through the fog. Following the twisted river road, we hit a small hill and saw a sign marked "Eagle Rock." The fog slowed us to a crawl.

Whispering, we rolled the windows down.

"Hush up," was murmured between the seats. Slowing to a creep we passed by a church, two stories high. Craning my neck to see its name, I was crestfallen.

"It's Eagle Rock *Baptist* Church." There was a shroud of light ahead. Barb saw it first.

"Eagle Rock United Methodist Church. Wow. They have a lit church sign. This is it." Whispers filled the car:

"Red brick."

"Pretty good sized"

"It's on Main Street."

"The Annual Conference Journal says it has a hundred and some members. About twenty attend worship. Do you think we'll be able to find the other three churches?" I asked. We crawled past the town diner on the left, and less than ten houses on the right. Suddenly the town was gone.

"The other three ought to be north of here," Ted said. Squinting at the map by the dim dashboard light, I tried to find their names.

"No, they're not on the map."

"Maybe this is one of them." Barb pointed to a gravel drive that went straight downhill ending at a clapboard church. "No sign."

We all sighed. The darkness and the fog overcame us.

"We need to head back," Ted and I agreed. Tomorrow morning we'd be driving to Hampton—which was five hours away—in order to get set for our wedding

"An hour and a half, one way, over the mountain to my closest church," I said gloomily. "My churches are not really 'near' to your churches like the superintendent said."

By the next afternoon, we were driving through Hampton and stopping at Fort Monroe.

"Here it is, Barb," I pointed out the gazebo on the lawn near the water. "This is where we'll have the ceremony."

"It's beautiful," Barb said in a hushed tone.

ॐॐॐ

"Well, we're off to the beach!" Ted announced with anticipation. Weaving our way through the tangled web of interstates that connected the tidewater area, we soon arrived at the beach. We scrambled out of the car.

"Race you to the beach," I challenged everyone. Up the boardwalk, down the stairs, and onto the beach we tumbled together. "Isn't it great?" I asked Barb. She nodded as we kicked off our shoes and headed for the cold surf.

Two days later we were married with my family there in support of me. Four days later, we were honeymooning in my grandfather's cabin in Wisconsin.

Back in Virginia, I drove to Roanoke to meet with the superintendent. He had not told anyone at the four churches my name. He was afraid that if they heard their new minister was a woman married to a black man, the church members would rise up and insist someone else be sent as their pastor.

"What's the best way to do this?" he asked as he leaned forward over the desk.

"It's much harder to reject someone once you've met them face to face," I said.

"Okay. I'll set up a time and we'll go next week," he said and leaned back with relief.

The day arrived. We rode the forty minutes north of Roanoke up the valley and arrived at Eagle Rock UMC. Inside, I was excited to see a large sunny room. A circle of folding chairs were waiting with refreshments nearby. But only the afternoon sunshine streaming through the window seemed at ease.

The head honchos had gathered. Suspicion hovered in the air like so many dust motes. I could see the questions in their faces.

"Why didn't they tell us the new preacher's name before now?"
"What is wrong with this situation?"
"Who's trying to pull a fast one over on us now?"

"Hello, everyone. Thank you for coming out today," the superintendent extended his greetings. "This is Teresa Smith, your new minister."

I greeted them with a smile and a warm handshake. Punch and pound cake were served with questions. The superintendent answered most of them.

"Teresa just graduated from Emory University. Her husband, Ted, is a minister on the Lynchburg district." He didn't divulge specifics.

"What about housing?" the Glen Wilton UMC representative asked with raised eyebrows.

"She'll be living in her husband's parsonage," The superintendent assured them. I smiled but thought, *There's no way I'm commuting three hours a day.*

"Tell us about yourself," requested the schoolteacher from Eagle Rock. So I did. Tentative smiles appeared when I said I'd grown up on a farm with five brothers and sisters. Within an hour, we were riding back down the valley. The superintendent relaxed and chatted as he drove; his work was done.

The week sped by. Wednesday afternoon Ted and I showed up for my first day on the job; a meet-and-greet reception open to anyone from the four churches was held at Eagle Rock UMC. The chairs were circled again. Ted stood in their midst. He was Reverend Smith, from the Bethany-Ebenezer Charge in Lynch Station, Virginia, over the mountain. But his brown skin blinded many of them to his personality.

"Where's Callie?" someone asked Robin, a leader at Eagle Rock. She sidestepped the question. The conversation turned to pound cake.

"Callie makes the best pound cakes," Robin shared with me.

Within days, racism's myriad forms rose in my midst. Callie couldn't get over my interracial marriage, so she stopped attending church. Jeremy took to sitting in the back pew of his little church. During the worship service he drew cartoons on his bulletin and mimicked politeness.

Every Sunday, I would run the route. I would start preaching at one white clapboard church on the backside of a dusty gravel road, Bethel. After the nine o'clock service, I went around the side of the mountain and across the river to the isolated community of Glen Wilton. Following the ten o'clock service, I drove down the highway and across the James River into Eagle Rock for the eleven o'clock service. The fourth church, Shiloh, rotated with the other three so each had worship services three Sundays a month.

One day as I sat in the office at Eagle Rock with the space heater buzzing, filling the room with a dusty burning smell; the phone rang.

"Hello, this is Reverend Teresa Smith."

"Is this Teresa?" came the querulous voice.

"Yes, this is she."

"Mabel, here. Young Jenkins is in the hospital. He has cancer."

"Okay, I'll head over there in a few minutes," I responded. There was a pause on the line before she continued.

"You need to know Julie has stopped coming to church."

"Oh," I tried to be neutral in my response.

"Says she won't come back as long as you're our preacher. Thought you ought to know."

"I'm sorry to hear that," I said as my heart split, and my stomach curled into a tight fist.

"I can't believe she's acting this way. Everybody's upset about it! I think we should have the superintendent come," Mabel said with certainty, righteousness, and a bit of anger.

"Thank you for calling and letting me know. I appreciate it," I told Mabel.

When I hung up the phone, I dissolved into tears of anger and hurt. Once I'd rinsed off my face, I locked up the office. I had a hospital visit to make.

The thirty minute drive to the hospital gave me too much think time. Mabel wanted me to call the superintendent to mediate. Humph. Call the one who didn't know how to tell the people that he was sending a good solid minister and they'd appreciate it? Expect that he would be helpful? I didn't think so. I was loath to call attention to the racism so that the "I told you so's" would rain down.

It was eating me alive. Who could I talk to about the unending racism? Ted? No. This was old hat to him. It wasn't personal for him. For me, every blow was new and unexpected. Karen? Yes! My old roommate, I trusted her.

I arrived at my conclusion at the same time as I arrived at the hospital.

Passing the nurses' station, I headed to Jenkins's room. Bible in hand, I knocked on the open door. Jenkins looked at me, then turned away. I stood in the doorway.

"I'm Teresa Smith, the new preacher from Glen Wilton. Mabel told me you were here, so I came by to visit."

Jenkins didn't look at me. I'd heard he was against my marriage.

From the doorway I asked: "Would you like me to come in and pray with you?"

No response. No acknowledgement.

I wondered what to do. A nurse approached with a medicine cup.

"Mr. Jenkins?" she asked.

"Yes," he answered.

"I have your pain meds here," he smiled at her. He took the meds and joked with her. She went back to the medicine cart to help the person next door. His face went blank and he turned away from me.

"Mr. Jenkins, I'll be going. If you'd like me to visit, give me a call." Silence. Within minutes, I was back in the car weeping. How could someone think it was wrong to love another person?

That night I called Karen. She listened and listened and listened. The tight fist in my gut loosened. I thought I was okay. Mere hours later, it was back. I was haunted by the rejection and racism.

I thought over my conversation with Karen. "Do you love the people?" she had asked me.

"Yes, I do, but I don't know what to do with them!"

Once again, I was the fourth grader hidden in my bed with the pillow over my head, sobbing to God. Asking God to take away conflict and injustice, I prayed that God would hear me, fix it, and love me. How could I preach to these people when I was so angry and upset?

෴෴෴

"Will you open us with a prayer, Teresa?" Robin asked. My first Personnel Committee meeting came to order. "The first order of business is housing. Teresa would like to be nearer to us, rather than trying to pastor full time from such a distance."

"But the parsonage is rented out," Dewy stated.

"I'm not asking to live in the parsonage. Perhaps we could rent a small apartment nearby. I've found one in the old Victorian house near Fincastle. It's a little more than two hundred dollars a month," I shared with them, blushing.

"If the apartment is adequate, then I am in favor of it," responded Carol.

"Is there a motion?" Robin inquired.

"I move that we equally divide the rent between the four churches in order to secure an apartment for the preacher as of next month," Dewy said, hoping to get home in time to catch the football game.

After the vote Robin said, "Our next order of business is to determine how things are going within our churches. Is there anything that needs to be addressed?" The room was silent.

"I have a pastor's report," I spoke up. "I'll continue having office hours from nine to eleven. I've been making weekly visits to those in the nursing home. Here's the list of shut-ins that I have been given. Are there others who should be added?" I asked.

"I'm shut in all the time," Jeremy joked. Everyone laughed.

"Anything else we need to address?" Robin asked. One by one, people began to examine their shoelaces and pocketbooks. "We'll close with prayer," and with that, Robin adjourned the meeting.

Back in Lynch Station on my day off I asked Ted, "Want to go for a hike and a picnic, after the car is fixed?"

"Sounds good to me," he said with a smile. At three o'clock we got back to the house and I searched through my stuff for my sneakers.

"Wretch!"

"What is it?" Ted asked from the living room.

"My other sneaker is over in Eagle Rock," I said flatly. The phone rang. "Hello? Ted, it's for you." I watched his face as he talked.

"Tonight?" he exclaimed. "Argh. Okay, I'll see you then." He hung up the phone and turned to me, "I'm sorry. I forgot I have a meeting tonight. Let's go to the Leesville Dam instead." We waded in the cool water, but I couldn't let go of it.

"How can you not remember when you have meetings?" I grumbled. Ted simply shook his head and pulled out our picnic basket. This conversation was a rerun of a rerun. We finished eating our fried chicken. Ted got out the Frisbee.

"Great throw," I said as the Frisbee looped, spun, and landed at my feet. The water beckoned us, but off we went so Ted could get to his meeting on time.

"I should be back in an hour," Ted said over his shoulder, as he strode out the door. By half past ten I felt ornery all over again. No Ted. I wrote my frustration out in my journal. *After being engaged and living apart for a year and a half, we are still not living together. When I am on his side of the mountain, he has work to do! I keep having abdominal cramps. Is it stress?*

Within minutes, my brain was in a spin cycle. *People hate me for marrying a black man. I must be doing something wrong or they would understand. How can they not see love is of God? I must be doing something wrong. I can't ever do anything right. I've never been able to do anything right. It's always wrong. I might as well be dead.* Spinning. Spinning. Spinning. The thoughts whirled around in my head. I dissolved into tears, until sleep overtook me.

Every week the smell of urine greeted me as I entered the nursing home. I walked the gauntlet past women and men bound up in wheelchairs and the past.

Their refrains, "Help me. Help me. Help me," and hands grabbed for me as I walked by. I was going to visit ninety-year-old Grace.

"Hello, Grace!" I said cheerfully.

"Take me home," she ordered me. "Take me home."

"Shall we sing some songs?" I asked.

"Take me home. I can't sing any songs." She gripped my hand tightly with her seemingly fragile hand. She had an iron grip.

"How about 'Amazing Grace'?" I persisted

"No. Take me home. I can't sing. You go ahead."

"Amazing Grace how sweet the sound, that saved a wretch like me . . ." I sang. By the second stanza she joined in with me. At the end, she slapped my knee and gave me a huge smile.

"We did it!" she fairly crowed with pleasure. She had forgotten about going home, because in the songs, she was home, I thought.

I had visited Will next. Will followed me with his eyes but didn't speak. Mrs. Etta had Alzheimer's and didn't seem to notice when I visited her. I trudged out to my car and drove over the mountain past bony, dry cornstalks, followed by a howling wind, home to my new husband.

By the next morning, I was leaning against the front porch in tears. An odd car sped by. But it was basically a lonely place.

"Let's go to the mall," Ted suggested; he was sitting on the steps. "Or how about out to eat in Lynchburg? We could stop in and visit with Mike and Linda."

I slid to the floor. "Those are your friends! I don't have any." Suddenly, I sat up straight and gave him a fierce look. "I just drove an hour and a half, one way. I don't want to get in the car again." We went nowhere, did nothing except order pizza.

In bed that night, the spinning thoughts took over my brain again. The rhythm was the same, but the words had changed: *I have no friends. I have no life. I can't even be nice to my husband when I see him. I might as well be dead.*

I wrote in my journal.

> *October 4, 1988. Death all around. Dying people, cancer, dialysis, heart conditions, accidents, dying people. Depression, bone deep. Help! I'm only twenty-five years old. I'm supposed to be experiencing life and hope and be in ignorance of death.*
>
> *Why must people like Bud Smith die? Why must Bill suffer? Why, oh God, why? I'm afraid there's no satisfactory answer. Not a single one in the universe. How can one believe in life when death is so damned predictable?*

Lu Ho is what Ted called the man. I had gone to the pastoral counseling center for help. Every week I went to see Lu Ho. He was my only friend, but I must pay him to be my friend. He didn't say, "You are depressed." I didn't say, "I wish I were dead." The weeks crawled by.

Lu Ho could figuratively hold my hand but was unable to grasp my thoughts. I took myself to the public library. I read book after book covering grief, death, being widowed, psychology, and spin cycles. Spin cycles were integral in my life; I regularly beat myself up by over-thinking negative thoughts.

Immersed in the words, I found solace. Embedded in the books were words of compassion, explanations of Kübler-Ross's stages of grief, and exercises for over-thinking. Alone in the apartment night after night, I practiced the exercise for stopping over-thinking. Gradually, it began to work.

A member of Glen Wilton, Dana's husband suffered from Alzheimer's disease. After I visited him, she and I went out for Chinese food.

"Ready for supper?" Dana asked.

"Sounds good. How's the week been?" I asked as we drove off.

"You know," Dana said. She gave me a knowing sideways glance. "I can't believe this is happening to me. How could it be that you could lose your memory before you turn sixty?"

"I've been reading about the stages of grief. To face change is to grieve. One of the stages is disbelief. That means you're normal," I said with a smile.

She burst into a smile, "I don't think I have ever been called that before. Honestly though, it helps to know."

Wood smoke held on to me like a dying man; I got into the apartment and took off my insulated flannel shirt. While I warmed up some soup, I got out my journal.

> *October 23, 1988. Exhaustion. Shiloh Church made seventy gallons of apple butter, cooked outside in a giant kettle over a wood fire! It's their one fundraiser each year. I helped peel apples for a good long while. They put pennies in the kettle of apple butter to help keep it from sticking on the bottom and scorching while they're cooking it!*
>
> *Bud Smith looks like death. My belly aches something awful. Cramp-like. I have been to see the OB/GYN and he's run tests but they're all negative. He asks me if I am receiving counseling, implying that the cramps are psychosomatic. I'm insulted. Is he saying I'm crazy? Yes. I'm seeing Lu Ho, I tell him.*

∽∽∽

Four days on my side of the mountain, three days on Ted's side. Rarely did he make the trip over. I couldn't say I blamed him. The smallest thing sent me off on some rampage. I journaled.

> *December 9, 1988. Why are people such jerks, so inconsiderate? If it's not logical then it's not worth listening to you. Forget it! I said, Leave*

it. Don't vacuum. I hate the noise. I'll do it later. No. That wasn't good enough. Vroooom. The damn machine. The stupid insensitive person and the damn machine.

We put up the tree and I cried. Every year for as long as I can remember as the tree was being put up I felt utterly alone. I felt like a spectator, not a participant. Every year I think I ought to be happy. I ought to be enjoying this. Every year I feel sad and alone.

This year after spending six months and seven years convincing myself I didn't care about being away from my family, I've concluded I miss them and all their horrid imperfections greatly. I want to open gifts Christmas Eve. It's our family tradition. But he can't see it. I guess I'm not showing him very well.

I hate it when I cry. I feel like a darn manipulative woman. That's not my intention at all. I cry because I'm sad or unhappy or hurt. Tonight I cry for lots of reasons. I wish I lived where Christmas was no more. I wish I had a secret hiding place. Oh, I feel like such a child.

Dear God, won't the hurt, the sadness, the tears, ever go away? Oh, please. I've spent a lifetime pleading and begging and hoping and writing and praying that you do more than sit here with me.

ოოო

I led Bud's funeral service. During his eulogy I said, "We will remember Bud when we eat boiled chestnuts. We'll remember how he greeted us from his hospital bed with jokes, stories, and a pocket of boiled chestnuts …"

"Teresa, I'm glad you could come by," Bud's family greeted me at the door of his house. "Come on in. Get yourself something to eat."

"Hello, hello," I greeted the church members perched on chairs and standing in knots around the room.

"Good job," one said.

"You remembered him exactly right," said another. Knowing that I couldn't leave without eating something, I got a plate. I placed token amounts of ham, green beans, and pound cake on the plate and looked for a place to at least stand out of the way. Balancing my plate on one knee, I tried to socialize, as expected. The emotional toll of preaching the funeral was overwhelming. I wanted to go home.

"How's the cattle?" one man asked another.

"Is the plumbing okay over at the church?" one of the trustees asked the lay leader. Above all the other voices, you could hear Violet, a church member.

Perched on a chair in her finest, she pronounced, "You just can't get good colored help anymore!"

I lost my appetite and moved to the kitchen to thank Bud's sister. Suddenly, Violet came rushing in. "I'm so sorry. I didn't mean to offend you. I didn't know," she gushed, her face bright red.

I murmured, "That's all right." Then I slid through the house like a ghost. Six months and nearly a dozen funerals had gone by. I felt like toast.

"Living in two houses, separated by mountains, isn't working for us," Ted told his superintendent. The superintendents began working on it.

Some of my people said, "Just send Ted up this way. We want to keep Teresa." Had they forgotten about the racists in their midst?

The phone call came. "Ted, we'll be sending the two of you to Christiansburg. Teresa will serve three churches; it should be a smooth transition since they've had clergywomen guest preach regularly. Ted, you'll be pastor of a church half-time and Chaplain of Ethnic Minority Ministries at the Wesley Foundation at Virginia Tech. It looks like you'll be able to live in the parsonage."

The following Friday, Ted and I did the preacher drive-by. We were shown the parsonage. We found Ted's church. But before we even began to pack, the news came.

My superintendent called me, "Teresa, it's not going to work. The churches are unwilling to accept a minister who is part of an interracial couple."

Later we heard that the smallest of the three churches had called the superintendent, "If you send that preacher to us, we'll close our church." When Ted and I heard about the threat, I exploded.

"What!" I sputtered. "In this day and age, the bishop will allow a church to call the shots?" I was angry that the system that proclaimed Christianity would allow racism to trump Christian values. *The Book of Discipline* said that United Methodist churches agreed to take whoever was sent as their preacher, regardless of race, gender, or ethnicity.

ॐॐॐ

I went back to see the OB/GYN again. The cramps hadn't stopped. I still got them at random times. No answers.

෬෬෬

March 10, 1989. I put on my overalls. I planted my bulbs. I pushed sod in the ruts I'd made when the car was stuck last month. Then I changed the oil in the car. As I was changing the oil, Ted reclined in the lawn chair, meditating over his sermon. The little girls from next door wandered over shyly. Their braids were numerous and their smiles infectious. They're all thin, dark legs and long arms.

"Whatcha doin'?" they asked.

"Changing the oil in my car."

"Why isn't he doin' it?"

"He's working on his sermon." They slyly glanced his way. Sure enough, his eyes were closed! Who works with their eyes closed? The girls disappeared through the hedge. I laughed and went to wipe the oil off my hands.

෬෬෬

The superintendents resolved the situation: Ted was sent to Christiansburg. I'd stay at the Eagle Rock charge. We'd live in between in Salem. Hurray! City living with its many options was a treat. Pizza delivery would be ours again.

SLAYING THE MONSTER

- How did Teresa take the ongoing rejection? Did she react or respond?
- What's the difference between reacting and responding?
- Do you believe that when we do not express our emotions about a situation, our body speaks for us through pain and injury?
- Name some positive things Teresa did that helped her.

MORE: BEHAVIOR MODIFICATION
AND FORGIVENESS INFORMATION

Behavior Modification is the process of making a change in your life, changing a habit.

Step 1: Recognize you have a habit you do not like. Good Job!

Step 2: Decide you want to change it. Think about why you do what you do.

Step 3: Map out a strategy to make the change. Choose the start date and method.

Step 4: Recruit other people to help you. Can you call them any time of day or night?

Step 5: When you feel yourself slipping into the old habit call a friend, take a walk.

Step 5: Forgive yourself when you blow it and start again.

Forgiveness is essential to the process, it works best with prayer and God and Scripture.

Assurance: God sent Jesus to say, "I love you!" (John 3:16). "There is hope" (John 1).

9

Matchmaker, Matchmaker

SEPTEMBER 1989. MY GYNECOLOGIST had finally agreed to *do* something. I was convinced I had endometriosis, a condition where the lining of the uterus grows in the abdominal cavity causing pain. He did outpatient, exploratory, laparoscopic surgery.

Less than two weeks went by; Ted and I were back at my gynecologist's office. This time it was a matinee movie. Hah.

"The surgery found nothing abnormal," the doctor reported. We watched the shadowy video of my insides; he pointed out my fallopian tubes and uterus demonstrating that there was no endometriosis. As we drove home I sighed over and over again.

Ted said, "Stop it!" I had gotten on his last nerve.

The surgery made it official. Lu Ho was not a good match for me. I told him I wouldn't be back. I didn't tell him why. I felt even more alone.

Fog blanketed the valleys on that fateful October day; a ministers' retreat for women was underway nearby. I'd come for the first day; the second day I had a funeral.

There, seated at a picnic table with a couple of other women was a tall, brown-eyed woman. She beckoned me with a smile.

"Come over. Take a seat. I'm Corrine, a college chaplain. We're doing introductions." After we'd gone around the table, Corrine said, "I want to start a clergywomen's support group that meets regularly. Are any of you interested?"

Several of us nodded.

We laughed and joked, "Yes, we'll create a support group for Corrine!" My friend, Haley, and I hadn't admitted that we desperately needed this group too. Thus began a three-year tour on Corrine's support group, it involved breakfasts and lunches every other week.

Weeks went by before I confessed, "I need help. I need a psychiatrist." Ted had given me an ultimatum. Get help or ...

Corrine had the answer, "Dr. Marnie Shields is the one we refer our students to at the college."

I made an appointment.

November 1989. Dr. Marnie's large glasses reflected concern. I had sunk into the chair. Everything felt dark.

"Tell me what brings you here today," she said in a clear alto voice.

My chin trembled and I began, "I can't stop crying. I've been mean to my husband. I can't get out of bed in the morning."

Then she said, "Tell me about yourself."

I wanted to turn sideways and disappear. I didn't want to open the past. It would hurt. Slowly, I opened the lid. The easy part was on top.

"I grew up on a farm with five siblings in Wisconsin." The underside smelled moldy and musty. It was damp from tears and excrement. "My dad used to hit my mother, fly into rages. I was afraid of him." The dam had broken. I was sobbing and shaking.

"I'm the pastor of four churches. People die all the time. I conducted twenty funerals last year. The churches and communities are small and the age of people in worship at two churches averages sixty-five. The other one isn't much different. The fourth one is on a dirt road with no plumbing and some kids."

"That must be hard," she said.

I nodded.

"Have you ever been on medication?" she asked.

I shook my head, "no."

"Are you willing to try medication?" Dr. Marnie inquired.

"No." My head screamed! *What? I am not that sick. My family pulls itself up by its own bootstraps. Are you saying I am mentally ill? Just tell me how to fix this.*

"Is there anything else you would like to share with me?" she asked quietly.

Dully I responded, "I am married to a black man. He is good and loving and makes a good living. My grandmother was heartbroken because I married him. My father has been teased about having a black son-in-law by the neighbors. My churches were shocked."

"So your professional life, your family life, and your personal life are all very difficult," she summed it up in a neat package as if to ask, "Is this yours?"

I nodded.

"I would like to see you next week," she said. My shoulders felt like they were dragging on the ground as I left her office.

The past had pooled around my feet like so much blood. No one could put the blood back into my veins; so as I walked out to the car, I left bloody footprints. At home, I went straight to bed, wrapped all of the blankets around me tightly. My head ached as if sharing the memories had required brain surgery.

༺༺༺

"Hey, Teresa!" Corrine called out. The little restaurant was packed.

"We're over here," Haley waved as she pointed to the table. We ate hot apples and biscuits, Famous Anthony's style. Laughter filled the table and bubbled up all around us. Haley joked about her green living room.

"My parsonage has the longest couch on the East Coast," she joked. "The living room has three chairs and the couch. Every one of the pieces is a different shade of green. Yellow green, moss green, blue green, and gray green!"

"This week I made three home visits all on the same afternoon," I shared "At the first house, I was served five-flavor pound cake; the second house, chess pie; and the third house, great-grandma's pound cake. Good thing I have dental insurance."

We lingered a long time, reluctant to leave this sunny spot, this circle of hope.

༺༺༺

Week after week, Dr. Marnie asked me the same question after I had filled her in on the number of funerals, the patronizing funeral guys who called me "Honey," and how I flew into a rage over Ted leaving a cereal bowl on the living room floor.

"Are you willing to try medication?"

By January, I was too weary to protest. My tears could have created another ocean. It seemed my chair in Dr. Marnie's office had a hole in it that I slipped down inside of when I visited her. She prescribed an old standby of an anti-depressant.

With every tablet, I ate resignation. My body had betrayed me. Surely it could come up with the missing brain chemicals if it wanted to; surely clinical depression belonged to someone else, not me. Six weeks passed. Eight weeks passed. No sign of change.

She weaned me off of that one, waited a week or so, then we tried another. She prescribed half doses for a week, then the full dosage. Six weeks passed. Eight weeks passed. May had arrived and with it a *no passing zone.* The anti-depressant had caused horrible constipation! Choking down prune juice hadn't changed a thing. She weaned me off that one.

In the meantime, Dr. Marnie had encouraged me to take a look at my inner child, as a way of learning how to comfort myself.

> *May 2, 1990.*
>
> *Dr. Marnie said I should imagine the child within, comfort her, and listen to her. Yesterday I could not even envision her. Tonight I coaxed her out. Hair standing up everywhere. Her first words to me, "Is it safe?"*
>
> *I searched the house I was born in, in my mind. No. Not the bedroom. It's not safe; I can still hear arguing. Not the living room. Finally she and I went outside, up by the pony shed. Princess looked out the shed's window. I rocked the little girl in my lap.*

I called home. Dad answered the phone. He tried to make conversation.

"Schumaker died, got his leg caught in the cornpicker. You remember Mabel Schutz, don't you? She has pneumonia. They don't think she has long to live." He paused for breath. "I was watching the grandbaby the other day. We were with the pony. The pony kicked him in the head and I had to take him to get stitches." Dad laughed! Then he said, "Well, gotta' go."

The phone clicked. Dad never said "good-bye" to anyone. I felt sick to my stomach as I thought about the conversation. Dad was the adult. He was supposed to be responsible, to protect and take care of my nephew. *Dear God, I thought after all these years maybe Dad could at least care for a grandchild, when he didn't care for me.*

ᭇᭇᭇ

The following week, I came home from meeting with Dr. Marnie and flopped down on our squishy couch to do my assignment.

July 25, 1990.

Seven days before menstruation. My nights are nightmares of depression. Six days before I'm in tears. I'm to chart my depression and my menstrual cycle to see if there is a correlation. That's what Dr. Marnie told me to do.

What happens? Small things upset me, situations I face every other day overwhelm me, I find myself longing to go away from everyone—to protect myself.

However, I've made a small forward motion. I called a speech therapist to deal with my hoarseness. An effort to value myself, to help myself, my voice. The guy hasn't called back yet.

In August, Dr. Marnie proposed the newest gee-whiz drug out there. Prozac.

October 1, 1990.

There are some days when I wake up now and feel great. It's hard to get used to feeling good. This a.m. I got up singing! Wild huh? This evening I'm practically in tears. Today I let my job get to me. I allowed what one person said and thought to take me for a nosedive.

Marnie said I should practice progressive relaxation twice a day for ten minutes. Somehow I haven't gotten around to it. Same thing with practicing my speech stuff. I've let it go for weeks now. Why do I do this? I need to make a change. I need to not let situations determine how I feel, what I think, and especially how I think of myself.

I made it through the annual report. "Life on this four-church charge involves great despair." Now that's encouraging! I've pushed myself hard to visit people at the little church and encourage them to make a decision about their future. I believe unless the two churches merge, both will be gone before the turn of the century.

Sad part is that some of the people have spent their entire lives fighting to survive. They don't know what life/ministry can be. I'm struggling to find some way to reach them. To help them choose life. Of course, that means choosing change. I must be crazy.

I keep telling them I'll accept whatever decision they make. But deep down I know if they don't choose life I will say, "Okay, superintendent, move me to another church if you can. There's more to life/ministry than sitting in despair." I don't want to manipulate them. But I can only take so much darkness, and despair. I know leaving won't remove my depression, but moving to a new situation sure as hell couldn't hurt.

O Lord, help me.

October 21, 1990.

As of Friday, 10 a.m., I had experienced hope and joy—real hope, real joy for what seems like the first time in my life. Two days later I could find a hopeful ending to my sermon. This is a landmark in my life.

The big events this week, which led to Friday involve
  —a letter of confrontation to Dad
  —one church beginning a Sunday School class
  —one church working to merge with another church.

I feel like a brilliant orange and blue butterfly.

Thank you, Jesus.

SLAYING THE MONSTER

- What problems did Teresa see, recognize, or have pointed out to her?

- Share a time when someone pointed out a concern he or she had about you. Or share a time when you recognized a problem in your own life.

- What are some of the ways Teresa addressed her situation? What ways have you used to address situations or problems in your life?

- How did Teresa practice her way into healing? How have you done this in your own life?

- What does hope look like for Teresa? For you?

MORE: FINDING THE RIGHT HELP FOR YOU

Matchmaking: finding the right doctor and counselor is important. Medication can give you the energy you need to make changes, while counseling helps you figure out what changes need to be made to live a healthy life.

The Counselor and the Client need to have a good connection. If your gut says it isn't working, find someone else. Counselors specialize in different types of therapies.

Some Available Therapies

  - *Talk therapy* (psychotherapy) helps you figure out why you do what you do, and how you think what you think contributes to your depression. Resources: Dr. Aaron T. Beck, www.psychologyinfo.com, www.undoingdepression.com.

- *Cognitive therapy* helps you work methodically to change habits. (Resources above).

- *EFT therapy* helps you create positive changes in your thought patterns through a series of talking and tapping. Resources: Dr. Gary Craig, author of www.emofree.com.

- *EMDR therapy* helps you create positive changes in your thought patterns through a series of talking things out with the counselor while hearing sounds and/or seeing flashing light patterns. Resources: Dr. Francine Shapiro, author of www.emdr.com.

Medication Matchmaking takes time, and trial and error by a psychiatrist to get it right. Pharmacologists are psychiatrists who specialize in brain medications.

A Supportive Network of Friends is essential to healing and long-term recovery. Harriet Lerner, author of the *Dance of Connection*, addresses how to make friends, what healthy friendships are like, and how to make and keep healthy boundaries.

Counseling, Psychiatrists, Friends, and Medication are gifts from God, through which God can bring healing.

Assurance: God calls some to be counselors; God calls us to seek help when in need.

- Paul counseled Timothy on what to do for an illness (I Titus 5:23).
- Moses selects counselors to help the people with decisions and disputes (Exodus 18).
- Deborah is called to be a judge and counselor (Judges 4).
- Jesus heals and blesses people when they have faith to seek help (Mark 5).
- Jesus responds when people call upon his name (Luke 17:11).

10

A Year of Hope

THE RED BRICK LIBRARY in Salem was less than a mile away. I was in hog heaven. If it had been possible I would have rolled around in the books. Lynn V. Andrews's books fascinated me, especially *Medicine Woman*. They made me think, reflect and journal.

> *November 3, 1990. I realize I've been bound a very long time. Bound in that, slowly, I'm unknotting the chains of the craziness, the past, and the neediness that has bound me. Bound in that I'm "bound for the promised land" traveling with God.*
>
> *When I read the Bible, even when I substitute God for a male pronoun I feel disconnected from God. But Andrews's words "The Great Woman Spirit" fill a void. I believe God is male and female, yet the female side is oft left hungry and cold in the Bible and in my life.*
>
> *O Great Woman Spirit.*
>
> *Often I am impatient. I don't want to evolve. I don't want life to be a process. Shazam! I want to arrive. I want to work hard then suddenly arrive.*
>
> *Thank you, O Lord of Spirit and Life, for examples like butterflies. Perhaps Robin is correct. Perhaps suffering brings beauty, but I don't want to believe it.*
>
> *Oh, how each year is better than the last. Oh, how each year brings me closer to you, closer to your image within me. Closer to honesty, boldness, integrity, and Christ.*
>
> *O Great Woman Spirit, I give you thanks for those who have showed me how to untie that which binds me. I give thanks for those who stand with me as you show me the way and I become closer to you. I give thanks for a Great Spirit such as yours, which gives my life value and worth. Meaning and purpose. Beauty and suffering.*

I couldn't put the book down. Nor could I stop myself from writing out my thoughts and revelations.

November 5, 1990. I'm returning to life. I'm coming to find life within myself. Worth is what I am finding. God's own image is a part of me. Amazing. Is it my toes that are like God? Or my slightly rounded belly? Or all the love I have within? I'm not sure.

This is only a beginning. More than I could have ever dreamed of. To be deeply in love and deeply loved by a man. To find hope. To feel peace. I know that our love, my love grows through the seasons. I'm excited and eager to see how this new-felt peace, new-found hope will grow. It's fall. I plan. I plant. Crocuses. Tulips. Irises. I'm great with expectation of spring. I'm eager for winter's cool cheeks. I am alive. I am alive.

<center>~~~</center>

Andrews's words pushed me like one's breath forces a balloon to expand and take on new shape. I journaled more.

November 7, 1990. Who has power and why? I'm finally realizing that for someone to have power over me and my future means I must give them power. Who gives power? Who uses and abuses it?

I'm finally claiming power of my own. It's frightening and refreshing.

<center>~~~</center>

November 14, 1990. "Corrine! Helen! How are you guys?" I blew into the restaurant. "Everything's crazy! I'm so jittery today; I can barely hold still. Tomorrow I'm scheduled to see Dr. Marnie. Maybe the jitteriness is from Prozac. Maybe it's from excitement. Wait 'til you hear what's happening."

"Whoa. Slow down, Teresa," Corrine grinned and offered me a seat.

"What's going on?" Haley asked.

"I'm so excited about my churches I scarcely know what to do. I've said I'll leave unless changes are made."

Haley's serious eyes were round with wonder. "How much and what sort of change are we talking about?"

"Eagle Rock has made a resolution and asked that Shiloh consider merging with them. I believe merging is the best answer."

"The question is," Haley reflected, "Is it the only answer?"

"No," I admitted. "Better cooperation and regular activities in pairs between the northern two and the southern two are steps in the right direction. An increased awareness and support of mission would be an awesome change."

We shared the pros and cons over breakfast and went our separate ways. That night I wrote in my journal.

> *I feel we're at the threshold of a new in-town church. Exciting! Is this enough for me to stay for? My head's spinning with all of this commotion. Dear Lord, Great Woman Spirit, help me to hear your voice, to sense your presence in this great and awful din.*

ฌฌฌ

November 22, 1990. Thanksgiving Day: a great day for a pity party. Trying to talk to Ted was impossible. On holidays he wanted to be left alone. It was a strain living with someone who didn't process things aloud or enjoy company on the holidays. Humph. I dialed the phone.

"Hello?" My mom's weary voice was both a worry and a pleasure to my ears.

"Hey, Mom!" My voice was all chipper. "How are you? Happy Thanksgiving!"

"Well, hello," she said with obvious pleasure, then sighed. "We've cut wood this morning and cleaned the barns." Her voice became upbeat, "The turkey's in the oven and we'll be at Grandma's house in a few hours."

I pictured the white tablecloth, wineglasses, fruit salad, and punch.

"What's new with you?" she asked.

"Gloom and doom. Elva All died. I have the visitation tonight. The funeral's on my day off—Friday. I don't want Elva to be dead. I loved her," I said, filled with pity for myself.

"I'm sure you'll be a great gift to them," Mom said with confidence. We talked about other things, then both rang off to get our dinners ready. Barely had I set the phone down when it rang again.

"Hello?" I said with weariness.

"Hi," My sister's voice said.

"What's new with you?" I asked with more enthusiasm than I felt.

"I can't believe you did it again!" she scolded. "What were you thinking? You send Dad these letters of confrontation and then we get dumped on. Aren't you just like Dad, dumping on people?"

"I can't control what Dad does," I said, with a chill in my voice. All the while I longed for a *new* family filled with unconditional love and understanding instead of this dysfunctional crap. "How can you call confrontation and direct communication 'dumping'?" I asked her.

"Okay, okay," my sister said with defeat, "I'll get this thing in perspective."

I hung up the phone, gave one of the couch pillows lying on the floor a good swift kick, while declaring: "I hate holidays!"

The pillow flew straight up. *Smack!* Glass showered down around me. I had hit the light fixture with the pillow.

❧ ❧ ❧

After the visitation, I wrote out my day.

> *Today I have said to myself Marge Piercy's words from her poem "For Strong Women"—". . . nag, ballbuster, bitch, nobody will ever love you back." Today I have thrown things and hit and cussed and taunted and wished for death and still, O Giving Mother, you love me in the midst of my pain and sorrow.*

❧ ❧ ❧

November 24, 1990. Ohh, the bed was warm. I started the day with prayer,

> *O Great Woman Spirit, I offer up to you blessings and gratitude for seeing me through this week safely. I offer you myself, and my love. Because of Ted, because of you, I have hope. Hope against hope. Thank you. Thank you. Thank you. Thank you. Thank you. Thank you, Mother of the Earth.*

December had arrived in dismal Virginia. No snow Virginia. I had finally figured it out. For years I had longed to run away. From what? *Me.* Why did I want to run away from myself? I tried to figure it out. I worked to create a realistic view of myself and my life. First, I listed the physical attributes I proudly accepted:

- My freckles are good, girlish almost.
- My nose is truly my mom and dad!
- My smile is worth a million bucks, Zola says. I do like my smile.
- Physically strong and proud of it.
- I like my blue-gray-green eyes.

- My feet are small and nice.
- I like my height because it's medium.
- My hair's a nice shade of brown.
- I even have a couple gray hairs for character.

~~~

Let's see. List my personal accomplishments. I couldn't think of any. The book I was using said to list some past hardships and put them into perspective with laughter. I gave it a shot.

- Okay, so the churches didn't merge. I learned a wealth of things in the process.

Next, I was to list instances of personal courage.

- Stood up to the church bully when he said I didn't do any work.
- Sent a letter to Dad concerning abuse.
- Had the courage to get counseling, do away with bad/abusive relationships, and to begin to heal.
- Went for what I believed was best for me in spite of opposition.
- Had the courage to go to Atlanta and the courage not to get sucked back into the cycle of family abuse.

Then I was to list the times I had chosen to take a risk.

- Married Ted and am a stronger, better person, and happier because of it.
- Visited guy in prison—if I could visit him, I could visit anyone.
- Confronted people about church's future.
- Stood up for myself when it was unpopular.
- Beginning to wear pants to work—don't need skirt/dress anymore to feel authority.

ལལལ

Four months of Prozac. It had been a vertical climb out of the pit while engaging in hand-to-hand combat with old habits and family systems the way they have always been. Each step of the way I had to consciously make choices to think in new ways. The Prozac had slowly refilled my serotonin reservoirs so that a bad day didn't immediately throw me back to the bottom of the pit. It helped me "pause" before speaking.

Before medication, when under stress I would blow up at Ted over stupid, irrelevant things. Step One: Blow up, yell, scream, get in his face. Step Two: Simmer and stew, ignore the person, leave the room, go and do something else. Step Three: Sob and reflect on the wrongness of the blow up. Step Four: Beg and plead for forgiveness for the wrong.

When depressed, the blow-ups startled even me. I had no idea where they came from and couldn't see them coming. Suddenly, they were there in full bloom. There was no thinking involved, only idiotic reacting.

With the Prozac, it was like my brain had a yellow light, not just red and green lights. When the light went yellow I took a moment and *thought* about the situation, then most times I handled it appropriately. I chose a response instead of reacted.

Nine months with Dr. Marnie helped me learn new ways of thinking. I no longer focused in tightly only on one small thing—the dirty dish on the couch—now I saw the bigger picture. Was the entire room filled with dirty dishes scraping against the ceiling? No. It was one bowl. Was I happy with my husband? Did he treat me lovingly or was the dirty dish one of a million awful things that happened in our relationship? She'd lent me her viewpoint and helped me to see differently. She had taught me ways to respond, as well as ways to go back in the past to care for myself and find healing.

Nowadays, breakfast at Famous Anthony's with Corrine really rocked. There was no quiet at the table. Rarely was I pensive and silent. Joy radiated from my face. When our day off arrived, we had a plan and friends who hung out with us for the day.

ལལལ

"Merry Christmas!" Ted's mom said to me over the phone.

"Merry Christmas to you," I responded. After the call I got out of bed and washed every dish we owned because every one of them was dirty! In between the dishwashing I made waffles just for me and ate them with real maple syrup. What pleasure.

By half past eleven, Ted had returned from delivering a food box to a lady in his church. We were off to Beth and Gary's house. As we got out of the car, we could see our breath in the frosty air. First, Gary introduced us to gingersnaps eaten with cheddar cheese and we drank hot spiced cider. Then, Ted and I snuggled in the big papasan chair and held their baby, in front of a roaring fire.

Later, over supper, Gary said, "Pass the ham,"

"Wait, have you had enough turkey?" Ted joked.

"I want more sweet potatoes and stuffing, please," I grinned and held out my plate.

"Do you want cranberry sauce too?" Beth asked.

I nodded with pleasure. "How about some cranberry apple pie?" she asked us.

"Mercy! Have mercy on us!" we cried out. "We'll eat it later!"

"Okay, let's go find the perfect Yule log!" Gary led the charge. The adults surged out the door. But Ted and I stayed snuggled up in front of the fire while the baby napped on Ted's tummy.

Hardly had the Yule log began crackling on the fire when the fierce competition broke out.

"Name the capital of China," Gary read from the game card.

"Beijing," Beth answered rapid fire. Gales of laughter swept across the table as Ted made attempts to draw things for his partner to guess. With Beth as my partner, we were sure to be the winners.

Back home on our night walk, I said to Ted, "That was the best Christmas ever."

He squeezed my hand and smiled. We were on vacation for the whole week.

"Oh my gosh!" I exclaimed. "I'm laughing at your jokes again."

"It's been a long time since you've been able to catch the humor in things," Ted observed. "I'm glad you're laughing again."

In some ways it was as if I were being born for the first time, tasting life and hearing things for the first time. I caught myself humming, hips swaying, dancing around the dining room table. I felt like the toys must have felt when they came alive in the "Nutcracker," limber and light. Light caught dancing in a rainbow prism—this was me.

There was no sermon to write, no funeral to plan. Deep sigh. No weight lay heavy on my shoulders. The tension of the year had melted away.

❧❧❧

"What did you preach on this morning?" I asked Ted after Sunday dinner. He told me about his sermon, and I told him about mine.

"I preached today on the Magi, how they followed God's directions and the star. I preached about how our sign is Christ. Then I asked the congregation, 'Will we journey toward life with Christ or stay behind?'"

"Do you want to go for a long walk, after we take a nap?" Ted asked. It sounded good to me. That evening we watched "Good Morning, Vietnam" with Robin Williams while I finished sewing Ted's bathrobe and repairing his clergy robe. I finally felt a sense of peace within—a certainty that God would show me the way. Either I would stay at my present churches or go elsewhere. The anguish was gone. It was like the sea after a great storm—calm and quiet.

❧❧❧

I walked into the office for our January meeting with trepidation; would I be able to speak my mind? My superintendent turned on his Southern charm.

"Teresa, you are a *very* independent woman," he proclaimed, after meeting with me to talk about my churches and the coming year. Later in the week, I told Mom what the superintendent had said.

"When I went into labor with you, I drove myself to the hospital," she said. I laughed hard.

"My superintendent thinks *I'm* independent; he's never met *you*!" Then I joked with Mom about her independence. After the conversation, I was sad. One shouldn't need that kind of independence.

❧❧❧

"Sally, I'm here," I whispered loudly in her ear. I sat down next to the elderly woman in her hospital bed. Her smile was beautiful and fragile. I stroked her head, smoothing back her silvery hair. No children. No family, save one sister waiting for her to come back to their room in the nursing home. A hushed sense of peace and privilege came over me. Oh, the intimacy that dying brings.

Within the hour, I was visiting Sally's sister, Mary. I just sat next to her. The room seemed so large without her sister there.

At the next hospital north, I stopped in to see Mildred and Ashby.

"Mildred! Ashby!" I greeted the couple warmly, trying to conquer the fear in the room. Pencil-thin Mildred was more shaken than Ashby who had pneumonia. This would be Mildred's first time to sleep alone at home—what with her husband in the hospital and her sister having died not so long ago.

On to the funeral home I went. In the small chapel people were packed in, knee to back, side to side. The tears almost formed a river down the center aisle. In the coffin was John's twenty-one-year-old son.

After the funeral the next day, I drove to the cemetery. The icy wind blew hard enough to wrench coats open. There on the mountainside, grief was as sharp as a knife. During the committal there wasn't anything I could do but hold John's hand tightly.

"I'll miss my brother," John's eight-year-old son said. We sat on the bumper of the Cadillac together.

"Are your ears cold?" I asked.

"Some," he said. I gently pulled up his hood.

"If you ever want to talk or have questions, you can always ask me," I said softly.

His "okay" was taken by the wind. The relatives embraced the dad and wept. The mom stumbled across the frozen ground clinging to a friend. But the eight-year-old and I sat on the bumper and stared. He stared at the casket. I stared too.

Driving the hour-plus trip home, the early dark of winter engulfed me. The wind pushed my car. The house greeted me with dirty dishes overflowing the tiny kitchen and laundry crawling out of the basket in the narrow bedroom. I read my Bible and collapsed into bed.

Happy Birthday, Teresa, I thought as I drove to John's house the next morning. I spent the day feeding the ducks and simply being with them. I couldn't imagine what it was like for them to have buried their son yesterday.

※ ※ ※

"Are we ready?" I asked Ted.

He answered by saying, "Let's pray. Dear God, watch over us as we travel. Amen."

Off we drove to Myrtle Beach, South Carolina, to stay in a timeshare condo. Monday evening after a good supper we opened the condo door and practically gasped! Talk about hi-class décor, topped off with bedroom and living room balconies placed so you could see the ocean.

A late-night stroll on the beach was followed up by time in the jacuzzi and swimming. We had to listen to an hour-long sales pitch in order to stay for free, but it was fun. For the first time in our lives, Ted and I could say we'd like it, we'd enjoy it, and we could *afford it!* But we don't want it.

Wednesday we packed up and headed south to visit Karen, my old roommate. We visited Epworth Island. The last night we ate at the Ole Plantation on Jekyll Island. The food melted in our mouths; there was even a wandering guitar player.

SLAYING THE MONSTER

- Have you ever felt hopeless? What was it like?
- How do you define hope? Recall a time when you were alive in hope.
- Hope and joy are entwined. How do you see this in Teresa's life?
- How have you experienced hope and joy in your own life?
- What did Teresa have to do to reach hope?

MORE: HOPE INFORMATION

Hope is a certainty inside of you that life can be better. It's not a destination, but a process and a possibility. It's the opposite of fear and doubt, giving up or giving in. Vickie Girard, in her book *There's No Place Like Hope*, says *"Hope swings open the door to possibilities."*

Hope sees what can be and creates the energy to move toward the possibility. Hope believes in possibility, things unseen. Hope can be yours. John, chapter one, speaks of a light in the darkness.

Assurance: Christians live their faith in the hope of Jesus' return and God's glory in heaven. The Bible uses the word hope 291 times. Some helpful passages include: II Corinthians 4, I Corinthians 13, Matthew 12:21, Romans 2:7, 5:5, 8:28, Psalms 23, 77, 59, 100, and more.

11

Transitions Galore!

I WAS DONE. I didn't want to take medicine anymore. It wasn't making a difference for me anyway. I hated taking pills. I tried to work up a speech to make to Dr. Marnie.

"Hello," she said. I took my usual seat in her office.

"Hi," I said nervously, wrapping my arms around myself. I looked at the floor, out the window, anywhere but at her.

"What's new?" she asked.

"I don't think the medicine is helping me anymore. I want to stop taking it. I want to see for myself if it makes a difference."

"Teresa, what you have is a chemical imbalance. Your brain doesn't produce enough of the right chemicals to stop you from becoming depressed. The Prozac helps produce serotonin. The serotonin is part of what balances your moods and allows you to feel good. You may need to take medication for the rest of your life," Dr. Marnie said. Nonetheless, she told me how to wean myself off the medication.

Ted said, "My brain is drying up! I want to go back to school."

"Go for it," I encouraged him, as we snuggled on the couch.

"I've looked into it and I can enter Wesley School of Theology in Washington, D.C., and do a part-time doctor of ministry degree program over three years. It requires being gone four weeks a year for classes."

It wasn't long before his dream was crushed. Ted came home dragging. "The church doesn't want me to do it," he said. "They said I'd be gone too much."

His frustration with the church's decision, combined with the weight of working in campus ministry where funding was questionable every year, pushed him to say, "Let's move."

Without Prozac, I seemed to do fine. I was well enough to see the whole of my work situation and discuss some of the causes of my clinical depression.

Dr. Marnie said, "When you are surrounded by elderly people and death, as well as uncertainty about funding to support a pastor for the next year, it is natural to be depressed."

With a heavy heart I shared with my Personnel Committee my decision to move. Their faces were downcast. I knew their lives inside and out. I knew Robin's sneaky humor, Carol's laughter—not to mention the car she drove and her extended family—and Howard and Sarah's diplomacy. Their love fed my soul like springtime.

We'd been through rich times, when the churches had been filled to capacity and the singing sounded in the glen. We'd been through thin times, when money was a constant issue, and death all too frequent. History had glued us together and bent us into a beam of support. Now I'd proposed that we split the beam. The sound of the beam breaking was wrenching.

Ted and I'd practiced our speeches. We'd done our research. The superintendent had mentored Ted. He'd comforted me in the darkest hours when I was surrounded by death on the charge. However, business was still business.

"Hello, Gene!" we called out as we entered his office. Ever debonair, he rose with a smile at the ready.

"Why, Ted and Teresa, it's good to see you." He acted like we'd stopped by for a visit, not a business meeting. "What are you thinking about this year?" he asked.

"I want to go back to school," Ted said passionately. "I know appointments in my salary range in northern Virginia are scarce but that's where I want to go. Cut my salary. Send me wherever you need to send me—I don't care. I want to go back to school."

I picked up where Ted left off, "Gene, we really appreciate you and the way you've mentored us. Thank you so much. I know, since we are a clergy couple, it makes it tough to find churches that are close to one another. I'm willing to go where you send me, send me to my own church or make me an associate pastor—either is fine.

"Please though, send me to a place where there's life. I've been surrounded by death all these years; I need some hope," I said. Gene jotted down notes on his legal pad, murmuring that, yes, he'd heard us.

He said, "It won't be easy. There aren't a lot of pastors changing churches this year. I'll do my best for the two of you."

Finally I spoke up about the hardest subject, "Gene, you know I've been working with these four churches for four years. I've grown the smallest one, started a youth group, and worked on merging two of them. I've worked hard. As I look over the salaries of my colleagues in ministry, it is clear that I'm nowhere near what the average minister with four years of experience is, salary-wise. I've been at minimum salary all these years."

"Oh," Gene remarked carefully, leaning back in his chair.

"It would take a five thousand dollar increase to put me near my peers, salary-wise," I added.

"Well," Gene said with firmness, "I understand what you are saying. Like I said before, I will do my best for the two of you. Let's pray before you go."

Months passed slowly. Information trickled through the grapevine, large salary church appointments were taken care of first. We were on the bottom of the heap, appointment-wise. One night, as we headed out the door to play volleyball with friends, the call came.

Gene spoke to Ted first, "Ted, we want you to be the pastor at Roberts Memorial UMC in Alexandria, Virginia. We have great confidence in you and your abilities."

Ted was in shock, "Wow. Thank you so much!" This was a prestigious appointment to a historic African-American Church. The salary increase was five thousand dollars. The location was perfect. He listened as Gene told him the details. Then Gene asked to speak to me.

"Teresa, we have been working on things in the Cabinet and we want you to serve as the associate pastor of a church in northern Virginia." I was speechless. This was the first time I had heard anything that I might become an associate pastor.

"What about meeting with the senior pastor before finalizing the appointment?" I asked.

"You'll be able to speak to him in six weeks or so when appointments are finalized," Gene assured me.

"But, I thought that senior pastors chose and interviewed their associates. Shouldn't we talk to make sure it's a good match?" I asked with growing concern.

"Now, Teresa, if you don't want to go . . ." clearly, he was angry and feeling insulted, "you can always stay where you are. This is a good appointment. You'll receive a generous five hundred dollar increase. I've worked hard for you and you should be grateful." That ended the conversation.

I burst into tears. I'd been run over. Ted asked for nothing but location and received everything! When I said I would be open to being an associate, I assumed the process I'd heard about would be followed. First, the senior pastor would interview me with a member of the personnel committee. Then he (there were no women senior pastors in the Virginia Conference in 1992) would determine whether he wanted me. If he did want me to be his associate, I'd receive a phone call and have the right to refuse if I didn't feel good about the match.

Something wasn't right. What happened to the process? Who was this man they didn't want me to meet? Why didn't they want me to even talk to him until after everything was set in stone? And what's this about an extra dollar fifty a day being a generous increase?

ৎৢৢ৵ৢ৵৵

"I'm scared."

"What are you scared of?" Dr. Marnie asked me.

"I'm afraid of falling into the pit of depression after we move. I don't know any counselors or psychiatrists there. Is there anyone you can refer me to in northern Virginia?"

"You could call some of your colleagues in the area and ask for referrals," she said.

The idea of cold calling someone made me freeze up. How could I call someone I didn't really know? How do you talk to strangers or acquaintances? When would be a good time to call? How would I know that I wasn't interrupting them?

"I'm sure you'll figure it out," she said. Dr. Marnie's confidence in me would have to carry me through.

My heart was being yanked out through my throat. I was excited and thrilled to move, and sickened at the idea of it. What would life be like without Alma "putting on the dog" whenever I stopped by. Who else would fill the table with homemade pimento cheese, a dab of ice cream, applesauce she had canned, venison she had cut up, and some chess pie or pound cake? How could I live without Robin's wry sense of humor? Honestly, teaching in the mountains and calling it "teaching English as a second language," only Robin would think of that! Where else would I find men named Booty, Hansford, and Essie—all with hearts of gold?

∾∾∾

I ranted and raved about the lack of process and consultation. I was to be sent to be an associate pastor in northern Virginia in July. I took my anger to my clergywomen's group who met quarterly to support one another, worship together, and work to change the Virginia Conference to more closely resemble the Kingdom of God. They commiserated with me. They told me their stories of sexist treatment: being overlooked, underpaid, and patronized. Together we found humor in it. The laughter brought some healing.

Protocol was that two weeks prior to arriving at a new church, the incoming pastor would have lunch with a church member or two. The church always initiated the meeting.

I was finding that protocol was followed if you were a clergyman; but if you were a clergywoman there was no protocol.

Finally, I shared my concerns with a superintendent, "No one from the new church has sought me out."

He was kind and reassuring, then said, "Teresa, we are sending you to this church because they need a strong associate pastor. You are that person."

I went away wondering why they needed a strong associate.

We moved into the parsonage in a quiet part of Alexandria. A tulip magnolia tree graced the yard with its fragrant, purple blooms. The yard was quiet; but inside, the house was undergoing a great upheaval. The church had decided that the kitchen was inadequate and in need of re-modeling. We were grateful.

Our boxes went into the basement while we were awaiting the work. The work moved forward at a turtle's pace. But refinishing the hardwood floors made them glow like honey.

My mother-in-law had been renting a room nearby. We'd decided she could live with us, provided there were two bathrooms.

I told my friends, "I'm so excited that Ted's mom is moving in. There'll be someone to share the cooking with and I'll have someone else around the house to talk to, since Ted is such an introvert." However, when face to face with my mother-in-law I found myself tongue-tied; I couldn't even begin a conversation about cooking.

"Ted," I said. "Your mom has been here several weeks; but I hardly see her."

"She's always been like that. She likes her space," he said. Slowly, I began to understand what Ted meant when he said he was introverted. His mother was even more introverted. I came from a family that didn't have doors on two of the bedrooms and didn't use the bedrooms except for sleeping; the idea that one would lounge in her bedroom was alien to me.

I didn't know how to initiate conversations about important things with someone unless we had been friends for a long time. My mother-in-law, however, was gifted with certainty and great amounts of common sense.

One night we shared a meal of spaghetti.

"Is there enough pasta left for Ted?" she asked.

I responded cheerily, "No. If he wants some when he gets home after his meeting, he'll make some." I failed to say that he hated leftovers so there was no point in cooking for him.

"Well, he'll need dinner," she pronounced and got up to make more pasta. Every conversation with her felt like a battle; I didn't talk unless necessary. When I did speak up, I felt like I needed to defend myself.

I had screwed up the courage to call a colleague—one recommended by a friend of mine. Clara said if I were looking for a psychiatrist I should go see Roberta Gilbert; she taught Bowen family systems and was super. Dr. Marnie's office had been dark and roomy. Roberta's office was small and white with blue chairs and an easel. She started by asking me to outline my family of origin and their relationships! I had never experienced this kind of "therapy" before. Bowen family systems was designed to help a person see how one person's anxiety or issue affects others within the family or workplace.

At the new church, life was equally uncomfortable. I was shown to an office that had a desk and a file cabinet. That's all. Floor space dominated the office. Someone offered me a couch from the youth room with the stuffing coming out the end. The youth director was embarrassed by the situation and spoke to a couple of the movers and shakers. Before I knew it, there was money for office furniture and a lady to help me coordinate it.

Dan, the senior pastor was kind, loved history and people. He told me my areas of responsibility. It felt like he had said, "You are so young—don't worry your pretty little head about money and building things or personnel matters. You can work with the children, sweetheart."

He didn't say these things. But I felt patronized.

I took my irritation to Roberta. She showed me how the patterns of my childhood with my dad were being played out with the senior pastor. The senior pastor wasn't giving me orders like Dad, but I felt powerless. It was helpful to see the relationships drawn out. I began to think through better ways of responding. It was hard work.

Directionless, I felt like I was on vacation all summer. After preaching three times a Sunday, every Sunday for four years, becoming an associate was a piece of cake. Here I was with heavenly bell-choir music during worship, preaching once a month, and sitting in an office with heat and other people nearby.

�∿∿∿

Back home in Wisconsin, Barb moved in to care for Grandma Sweet. She had amyloidosis, an autoimmune disease. No more chipper voice. No trips for ice cream. The grandmother who had encouraged me and told me I was beautiful and important was dying.

The distance made things difficult but not as difficult as the distance in my heart. I'd discovered that our relationship would never go back to the way it was. I was growing up and seeing her through adult eyes instead of the eyes of a child where everything was clear and without complexity.

∿∿∿

It was like watching "Peanuts" on TV. I couldn't hear who she was talking to, but I could hear what she said. I was sorting through my mail, in front of the mailboxes outside the secretary's office when I inadvertently overheard a phone call.

"Hello, this is Ruth," she answered the phone in a frank, cheerful way.

The Peanuts sound came over the phone, "wah wah wah wah wah wah." Then I heard her sigh.

"I don't know where Dan is!" she said in an exasperated tone. "I never know where he is!"

Realizing she was saying this to a church member, and that she was talking about the senior pastor, I fled the scene. What to do? What to do?

Should I tell him? No. They were good friends. That would be tattling. Or would it? Shouldn't an employee be expected to be positive about the pastor, not ugly and exasperated? Wait! What about me? If she says that about him and he's supposedly a friend, what will she say about me?

Immediately, I went into "preserve Teresa" mode. In college when I had to deal with grinchy people, I made friends with them so I could influence them sideways instead of head on. I knew what I would do. I'd give her a detailed schedule of my whereabouts a month in advance every month. Let it never be said she didn't know where I was.

As fall approached, I knew if I wanted to see Grandma Sweet one more time I had to go soon. But I'd put it off, booking a flight for early November. I'd thought about calling her and telling her I was coming to visit, but I didn't.

The day before I flew out, Barb called. "She died today."

I was speechless.

"She stayed in bed," Barb shared, "I kept going back and checking on her. I sang hymns to her. It was a good death."

I was angry! Why didn't Grandma Sweet wait for me to come and say goodbye? Then I was heartbroken.

Returning home from the funeral, I curled up on the couch and wept. Ted leaned over me. Then kneeling beside me he gave me the second greatest gift on earth—the first had been himself.

He said, "Our life is good. Anything we do is only going to make it better. If you want to have a baby now, that's fine with me." Now I wept with tears of joy and sorrow. We had long danced between "yes" and "no" on the topic of having children.

∾∾∾

January fell into place and away I went to the Minister's Continuing Education event. The second night, I looked around the drab lobby and realized my senior pastor hadn't made it.

"Have you seen Dan?" I asked one of his friends.

"Nope. How're you doing?" One of my colleagues asked me. No one had seen him. Dan was Mr. Social. Hmmm. With that, I called the church.

"Hello, this is Ruth."

"Hey, Ruth, I've been looking for Dan and . . ."

"He came down with pneumonia, so he's at Fairfax Hospital," she shared matter-of-factly. I thought it was strange that no one had called me; as associate pastor, I was "second-in-command."

"Don't worry about it," Ruth continued. "Dan's wife called me. The week's all taken care of. You can stay at the event."

Returning home, I found decisions were being made as if I didn't exist. I chafed about this, but not for long. Entering the hospital intensive care, I became ashamed of myself. Dan's gray complexion, the machinery attached to his chest, and his wife's expression made it clear that his life was on the line.

Instantly, I had all the meetings I wanted to attend and more. I preached every Sunday, visited him every day and checked on his family. Life was spinning. Would he live? I began to understand those words spoken to me in June, "They need a strong associate pastor." It turned out that Dan had a twenty-year history of heart problems.

∾∾∾

With great joy, Ted and I boarded the plane for Wisconsin. We were going home to buy our first house, my grandmother's house, barn and land from her estate. Days later, at a family get-together we ate pizza, but the pizza disagreed with me. Never had pizza disagreed with me! I always agreed with pizza. It was the first sign that I was pregnant.

"Let's wait until the second trimester to tell people," Ted said. Finally, we announced it with great joy.

Right after the announcement a mover and shaker in the church approached me, "How could you get pregnant now? This is bad timing. We need you to be focused on starting this new project."

Others were more than happy for us.

∾∾∾

A death led to a burial at Arlington National Cemetery. I was six months pregnant and it was a sweltering one hundred degrees. The funeral coordinator looked me over.

"Will you be walking with the caisson?" he asked skeptically.

"Of course, I will walk." I said firmly. What did being six months pregnant have to do with walking? Then I wondered to myself, *What's a caisson?*

The horse-drawn caisson approached and the pallbearers lined up. With the casket secured in the caisson, we began to march uphill at a steady dignified pace. As far as the eye could see, white tombstones ran in every direction. Rows on the diagonal and horizontal—always rows upon rows—here death rested. Here I walked.

Some had never been to a graveside service conducted by a female pastor, let alone a very pregnant female pastor. After the service, people approached me like usual.

"You said it just right," one murmured. I wondered, did they think I would do it all wrong?

"You're the first female minister I've met. You do a fine job," another person said as we left the cemetery.

∾∾∾

The barn we had bought from my grandmother's estate needed painting—the roof did that is. We gathered supplies. I prepared to climb the ladder and join Ted, Dad, and Mom who were putting on the roof coating.

Ted came toward me. "I don't want you up there," he said.

I opened my mouth to reply but nothing came out. Thoughts ran across my brain like a flock of birds fleeing a storm. In my family, no physical condition was an excuse to not work. Was he telling me what I could and couldn't do? I was an equal-rights kind of woman! What would Mom and Dad think? Okay, so it's really hot up there—hot enough to fry an egg—but "I am woman, hear me roar!"

Gee, he really wanted to keep me, and this baby-to-be, safe! Is this what care looks like?

"Okay." Off I went to find a shady spot. I was the paint stirrer.

∾∾∾

The early morning sun had hardly appeared on October thirtieth when I climbed into the bathtub to ease my aching back. I felt a contraction. I waited an hour or two before telling Ted. At seven that evening we went to the hospital. The labor hadn't progressed much. Midnight came and went. The results from every exam were the same. Not fully effaced. Barely dilated. The doctor sent the anesthesiologist in to administer an epidural.

The doctor said, "That way you'll be ready if we need to do something more."

Hours later, the next exam found that while I was slowly dilating and the baby wasn't stressed, it was taking forever. The doctor, midwife, and nurse came into the room to meet with me and Ted. Ted sat up on the couch.

Dr. G. began, "We have a decision to make." He paused. "We could proceed with a C-section at this time . . ."

I interrupted him. "No. I don't want surgery," I said emphatically.

He looked to Ted, and then to the midwife and said, "We'll give it one more hour."

I began to pray harder than I had ever prayed before. I imagined my cervix fully dilated. I visualized it opening completely. Over and over again, I pictured it in my mind and prayed that God would make it so. Thirty minutes later the midwife and nurse came to examine me. They took a peek and could see the baby crowning.

One said to the other, "Let's not tell Dr. G. Let's surprise him!"

Dr G. appeared in the room as if by magic. He sat down to examine me. Then he stood and almost crowed, "Let's have a baby!" He even did a little dance. Our girl was born.

"She has black hair," I murmured.

"No, it's dark brown," Ted responded.

He took her and she wound her fingers around his. The moment was magic and the miracle was breathtaking. Our girl was here!

Thus began a four-year prayer vigil for me. Not a day went by that I wasn't torn about our girl being in daycare versus me being home with her. I asked God to release me from my calling to be a pastor so I could stay home with her. My call to ministry continued as strong as ever. Our girl was healthy and happy. Only I was chagrined.

A year later, restlessness was overtaking my life. I'd spent more than three years working with Dan. Twice he had been very, very ill and I had captained the ship in his absence for months at a time. But we didn't have matching visions or approaches to ministry. I was in my early thirties—looking for challenge and excitement.

"Okay, Ted, tell me again how to say it." I wrote down what he said.

"Just remember, Teresa, you are presenting yourself as competent, professional, called, and cooperative. Here's one way to tell the superintendent you want to change churches . . ." Ted patiently coached and collaborated with me.

Fully rehearsed, I entered the superintendent's office door, when Joe stood up and said, "I need to make a run to the ATM; you don't mind riding along with me and talking as I go, do you?"

I said, "No, I don't mind." But I did mind. He wasn't taking me seriously.

Joe quickly launched into his plan to move Ted to a different church and how close it would be to the church where I now served as an associate.

In the midst of his spiel, as he said, "So I want to move Ted to ..."

I interrupted, "Speaking of moving, I want to move churches."

His great rush of plans screeched to a halt.

"Why? Why do you want to move churches?" Joe asked in disbelief. I tried hard not to let my resentment show as I went through my talking points.

Ted's superintendent, Doug, had been an incredible mentor to him and had pledged to have me serve on his district when a church became available. However, the first rumor we heard back was that my superintendent had not spoken up for me as someone who wanted to move. I tried to lay aside the thought of moving and work on a plan for how I could serve another year with Dan, without burning my bridges.

The tulip magnolia tree was blooming gloriously the day I received the call from Joe.

"Would you consider going to serve a church in the adjoining district?" Joe asked. He needed an answer very soon. I did a "drive-by." The church was a beautiful brick building nestled in a lovely lot in a suburb. I researched their attendance and financial statistics. It wasn't encouraging. I called and told Ted about my research.

Dear God, what shall I do? Help me to truly hear you. I prayed, even as I celebrated. Mostly though, I danced around with joy. I would be the one leading instead of going in one direction while feeling pulled in another direction.

Picking up the telephone, I called the superintendent and said with a big smile, "Yes!"

"Good, Teresa, good," he responded. "We'll have to figure out the pay ... I think it's thirty-five thousand ... The church is dropping its salary because it has lost so many members."

As I placed the phone in its cradle mixed emotions rose up. It was a tremendous opportunity that I wouldn't turn down. The leap of five thousand dollars compared to my current salary was one of sheer joy; finally I would be on the level with my peers. Then I realized that this salary leap would place me ahead of my mentors—who had served more years than I had—but had not received the opportunity to serve a larger church or receive a salary commensurate with their male colleagues.

Later I asked Doug, "What does it take to give a clergywoman a position of leadership in a larger church?"

"The superintendent has to be willing to go out on a limb and saw it off . . ." in order for the rest of the Cabinet and the bishop to accept the risk of doing things differently.

As a person who believed in standing up for underdogs, I was uncomfortable being closer to the "haves." I'd always been on the "have not" side. I'd had no power, no justice, and no voice.

Exceptions were made again. Instead of waiting until the day we moved in to meet the church folks, Doug sent me to meet them more than a month before I was to arrive. The first meeting was held in a retired military man's home. I wore my conservative blue suit with a scarf.

"Reverend Smith, come in," his wife immediately served cookies and coffee.

Three men gathered with me: two older, one near my age. They stood.

"Welcome," they said.

"Good to meet you," I responded.

Thirty-two years old was awfully young to them, their eyes said. A white clergywoman married to a black man wouldn't be easy for some of their members to swallow, their solemn faces said. Still, they smiled genuinely and asked serious questions of approach and strategy, wanting to know how I would bring their dying church back from the brink of death.

"Tell us about yourself," invited the chair of the Personnel Committee. So I began the story with my Wisconsin childhood.

"I've also brought my resume. Share it with whomever you wish," I explained. "I'm very excited to be coming to Wesley and look forward to working with you."

Walking out the door, I smiled. My feet said, "I am confident."

"Give me a year!" said my arm as I confidently closed the car door. "Give me a year and they'll come to love me," I whispered to the night air. It had been so twice before.

❀ ❀ ❀

"What have I to fear? What have I to dread? Leaning on the Everlasting Arms. I have blessedness with my Lord so near . . ." The piano played brightly as the congregation sang with fullness that first Sunday. I fell in love.

With someone in her early thirties in the pulpit it was like a subliminal message being sent. "You can give your money to the church; it isn't dying." Giving increased. Attendance grew.

Oh yes. Attendance almost always grew when a new preacher came to town. Everyone wanted to be an "eyewitness" reporter on what the new preacher was like. But these folks came, and mostly they stayed.

Amelia, a woman who couldn't stop talking, started talking about how great the church was. "You ought to come and see!" She was a walking billboard, only a hundred times better.

One morning, the previous youth director came flitting through the church hallway. Flo had a gift for putting people at ease. Dressed in her shorts and tee shirt, she remarked, "Can you believe it? They are painting my bedroom so I'm sleeping in the basement and can't get into my room. This morning I realized all my bras are in my bedroom so I had to wear my swimsuit underneath my clothes!" Laughter tumbled every which way.

Three months in, one of the retired men stormed into my office. He stood framed by the doorway, in the afternoon sunshine. Dave's brow was furled. His military haircut said, "Stand at attention."

"I can't come to the meeting tonight, but I'm absolutely against the way financial decisions are being made around here!" Dave thundered. He went on at length, standing in between the door and my desk.

I listened intently while sitting at my large desk. It was the same kind of tantrum my dad would throw, except Dave was rational, direct and courteous. He was simply wound up about the issue. When he finished, I looked him straight in the eye.

"I'm glad you were able to come and share your objections with me. I'll share them at the official meeting tonight for you."

He took a deep breath, seemed to be taken off his guard, "Oh. Thank you," he said gruffly and marched out.

I began to visit everyone. Dee retired a few months after I arrived, I called her right away.

"Will you help me? I'm trying to visit everyone in the church but need someone to schedule the appointments for me. I want to know what vision people have for the church."

"I'd be glad to help," Dee said, and dove right in.

The secretary, Beverly, had been an assistant to a general at the Pentagon; she'd clearly handled very big and important details with aplomb. I was thrilled by her personal story—a girl from out west determined to become an Opera Singer. She did it! Traveled around Europe, before her voice gave out and she married, ending up here.

"Teresa, I came in as a favor to Reverend Gold. He needed someone and I'd just retired. So I became the secretary and before that … Well, thirty-five years ago the choir director walked off the job just before the Easter Cantata. Reverend Tang begged me to come and help them through Easter. I helped them through Easter," she said laughing, "and I never left."

Loyalty, manicured nails, nice fleece wear and great difficulty hearing: that was my beloved Beverly. If I talked to her and her back was turned, she didn't hear a word I said.

The months sailed by and Holy Week arrived. Thirteen-year-old Cay and nine-year-old Anne made paper butterflies with me to hand out in church on Easter Sunday. Square masonry nails, like those given out on Good Friday, represented the butterfly's body. My daughter sat at the table, then played under the table. She was two and a half. I hadn't taken Prozac for four years and I was experiencing joy.

SLAYING THE MONSTER

- Strength and hope are integral to healing. Prayer invites God into our lives. It also invites God's power to flow through us and in us. When did you see prayer at work in Teresa's life?

- When have you experienced prayer making a difference in your life?

- How can you grow in your prayer life?

- What will you do this week to grow in your prayer life?

MORE: PRAYER CHANGES THINGS

Prayer is the way we connect with God. We can connect by:

- Inviting the Holy to be present wherever we are, whatever we are doing
- Sharing with God our deepest desires, thoughts, wrongs, and our entire life
- Remembering that Jesus was sent to reconnect the world with God's love (John 3:16)
- Meditating on Scripture, one verse at a time
- Joining a prayer group, Bible study, or covenant group
- Creating art as a prayer
- Engaging in sentence prayers. Choose one sentence and pray repeatedly
- Using guided meditation, form mental imagery as a method of interacting with the Holy
- Allowing other to lay hands on us and pray for healing
- Giving thanks trusting that whatever we need will be done (Matthew 17:20)
- Using written prayers
- Following the prayer Jesus laid out for us—The Lord's Prayer (Matthew 6)
- Trusting the Spirit to pray for us (1 John 5)

Resources: www.ourprayer.org, provided by *Guideposts Magazine,* www .upperroom.org, provided by the United Methodist Church, and books written by Dr. Roberta Bondi, author.

Assurance: God longs to hear from us (Revelation 3:20). Jesus longs to share with us (Matthew 11:15).

12

The Journey of Suffering

I WAS TUCKED IN our home office struggling with the Easter Sunday sermon when the phone rang in a jarring way.

"Hello?"

"Teresa? Is this Teresa?" the caller asked.

"Yes, this is she."

"This is Flo. It's terrible news," she said. "Eugene and Julie's son died this morning in Washington state. He was shot. Eugene and Julie called me from the airport in Florida. They'd been visiting their parents down there. There was no way for them to get a flight to see Dan before he died." I took down the flight information, so I could meet the parents at their home later that evening.

Numbness struck my body even as my head began planning out the events ahead. How would I tell the congregation on Easter Sunday morning that one of their bright and shining youth was now shining in the Kingdom of Heaven? The phone jolted me.

"Hello?"

A brisk voice said, "This is Bill. There's a vicious rumor going on around here and I want to know if it is true."

I swallowed, then said, "What's the rumor?"

He continued, "They are saying that Dan is dead."

"Yes," I said as my voice wavered. "It's true." The conversation ended but my questions continued. Some of the people would arrive tomorrow for the festive Easter service and already know Dan was dead. Others would not know until I told them. How would I minister to both groups so that they were able to receive the gospel in light of the situation instead of being swept away without a lifeline?

"Ted," I groaned as he came into my office. "Something awful has happened. Dan, a seventeen-year-old from my church, was killed in a drive-by shooting."

"Oh, Teresa, that's rough," Ted said with sorrow in his voice. "What happened?"

I told him as much as I knew. Then we began to talk about how we should change our family vacation that we had planned to start on Monday.

"The funeral will happen around Wednesday," Ted speculated. "I know you were really looking forward to the rest. You've been running full speed ahead, all year."

"The two of you'll just have to go to the beach without me," I concluded. "I'll come down after the funeral."

Dan had been co-captain of the soccer team. The whole team was camped out on the front yard of Dan's house when I drove up that evening. When Eugene and Julie arrived we hugged them. Together, we prayed that Dan would rest in peace and that God would comfort and keep us through the night.

At church, the Easter Sunday service music would carry me into a place of great joy, but then I'd remember and be somber. Preaching the resurrection brought joy to those far from death. It brought assurance to those close to death. However, it did not remove the suffering or the questions families and friends ask when a young person dies.

The Easter Service ended.

"I am saddened to announce that Dan died yesterday," I told the congregation. An audible gasp rose from the congregation. Then a woman, who had lost her own grown child not many years before, dissolved in disbelief. After the service, men stood on the lawn in silent groups. Women gathered in the pews. Bewildered teenagers wandered. My family had left for the beach; I went home to an empty house.

Holy Week had been filled with services of remembrance: Holy Thursday celebrating the Last Supper, and Good Friday remembering the crucifixion of Jesus. Always a turbulent time for preachers, Holy Week required extra energy. It was all done so that the congregation could personally connect with Jesus Christ, his death and resurrection.

I had nothing left to give. Looking ahead to the visitation, funeral, and myriad of details made me weep.

As Psalm 121 says, *"I lift up my eyes to the hills, from where will my help come?"* I was alone in a dark place; I needed someone to talk to and was unsure whom to call. I was a "process-out-loud" kind of woman.

Monday began with the phone ringing. The Holy Spirit was preparing to blow new life into my crumpled body.

"Hey, Teresa! Wha's up?" My old friend, Gary asked. My reply startled him.

"Well, hey," he recovered, "I was going to be in town, could you do lunch?"

Gary literally came from the hills, near the Blue Ridge Mountains. I'd been alone wondering where I would get help and God sent help from the hills! Gary came and sat with me in the weak spring sunshine, and did one of the things Gary does best—cheered me on.

After lunch, I headed over to meet with Dan's family.

"He had a yellow ski jacket," his brother said. "We called him Banana Boy."

I listened to stories of Dan's life; I wrote them all down in preparation for the service. Then, a fierceness rose up in the family.

Eugene said angrily, "Dan's death won't be in vain. Something good has to come out of it." The family worked hard, certain they could prevent this from happening to someone else. They designed a program that would shape children when they were young. They would be ready to tell everyone at the funeral about Dan's Campaign.

Julie pleaded with me, "Please come back to the Midwest with us for the burial." I would have done anything I could for this family, but I had nothing left to give.

"I'm sorry. I can't go. I'll send a tape of the service to the pastor there. I'll call him, but I can't go with you." I couldn't bring myself to tell them about my crushed vacation and waiting family.

Heading back to the church to handle the details of the service, I stayed on the phone for hours searching for an available organist. Less than twenty-four hours before the service, God provided an organist from across the metropolitan area. The organist had known Dan as a child!

The grass was a surreal green and the yellow forsythia bloomed wildly on the afternoon of the visitation. There at the church, people lined up for hours to extend their sympathy to the family. The line stretched down the front lawn's long sidewalk to the parking lot as night fell. Words echoed through the line:

"Impossible."

"Unbelievable."

"What happened?"

Retired men directed traffic. A nip bit into the night, but no one left. Inside, the family insisted on greeting every person. Over a thousand people came to pay their respects and walk this short way down the long road ahead.

The following afternoon the funeral was held at the largest church in the area—pews filled, lobby overflowed, closed circuit televisions provided people in another room a way to participate in the service. Nearly twelve hundred people came. I preached about Jesus calming the stormy sea. We had been rocked and shaken by Dan's death.

Finally at the beach, I collapsed into the arms of my family. I reached for God in long walks by the water. I slept. But still I couldn't fully rest. Three days later we returned home. I watched helplessly as Dan's parents slid into a dark abyss.

After mere weeks, some folks told Eugene and Julie to "get over it."

Others said, "You have other children; focus on them." These words only served to make the darkness more painful.

Still others continued to cook meals for the family, took care of the onslaught of death-related paperwork, and kept tabs on the parents.

One of the gifts of the church was its preschool. A ministry to the neighborhood, the preschool allowed me to lead chapel with the children every week. I loved everything about the preschool. As the preacher I was tasked with day-to-day supervision of the preschool director who in turn was the one who hired and supervised preschool teachers.

When I invited the preschool children to come and sing, their liveliness and joy lit up the face of the congregation that thought it was going to die. Even better, some of the preschool families became regular members. Children's time during worship zoomed from a handful to a dozen. It was delightful and challenging.

Then May came to an end; the letter arrived. Our preschool director had chosen to take a job elsewhere. The Education Committee Chair and I immediately began to search for a new director.

The applicant was incredible, strong in faith, and had lots of experience. We were thrilled to hire Ms. Q. During the hiring process, we asked Ms. Q about her supervision experience and informed her that while we had good teachers, there was one who needed some attention. Little did we know what that "attention" would unleash.

∾∾∾

On Dan's birthday, the tennis and soccer team held a candlelight vigil. I met with the parents and listened and prayed. Their pew at church remained empty; their shell-shocked faces unsettled people.

People asked me, "Hasn't it been long enough?"

"How long can they go on this way?"

I researched grief and the effects of a murder on a family. The average family grieved for a couple of years; a family whose child had been murdered tended to grieve even longer, three to five years the statistics read.

As the family's pastor I entered my own process of evaluation. What happened? What hadn't I preached on? What portion of faith was missing that kept this family from returning to worship and their faith family? The family said it was too painful to return to the place where the casket had been.

Conversations about God centered on how the Good Shepherd, our loving God could allow such tragedy. I wondered. Did we believe if we were faithful to God, God would be faithful to us by doing what we asked? "Protect us. Keep our families safe from pain and tragedy." Before I got very far in my reflection, parish life rushed on.

The Sunday morning attendance continued to grow, filling most of the pews. Books I read on evangelism and welcoming the stranger said that visitors stopped attending a church if there wasn't pew space easily accessible. We moved the choir up to the chancel area to provide more seating.

Money flowed. Mission grew. Music swelled the place with praise. The children seemed to multiply overnight. At home, our girl was almost three with a top-knot of curls and a golden complexion. She took our breath away, the way she laughed and danced. Ted worked hard to lose weight and succeeded. Wow.

In the midst of the joy, Ted said, "Teresa, I want to change churches. I'm frustrated and want to leave before I become bitter," I said okay, and we climbed on the rollercoaster of waiting to hear where he would be sent. I was really excited because I thought if Ted were sent to a different church we'd move to my parsonage. I wouldn't have to commute!

"Ted," Doug said, "I have a great place for you. It's a challenging place with great potential. The deal breaker is, if you don't live in their community, I can't send you there."

Ted and I talked. We prayed. We moved. I hated the move because it meant I had to commute to my church with rush hour traffic.

I mourned deeply. I didn't know the neighborhood. I liked our old house and neighborhood. Ted's balance between church and family was blown out of the water between his personal drive, enthusiasm, and the church's great needs. We searched for childcare and settled on a daycare center with a charming charismatic director.

As summer had turned into fall it became clear the daycare center was in continual upheaval.

"I love the Montessori school," I told Ted. "Hands on learning is the way to go."

"You're right. It's the best thing out there but they require a child be potty-trained. Our girl isn't there yet," Ted said.

Potty training was soon achieved! We moved our girl to the Montessori type school.

In the meantime, the church preschool had geared up. Enrollment was full! Quite a turn around for a preschool that had almost closed a few years back. Ms. Q was excited about a phonics curriculum. She was working to bring all the teachers on board.

"Hello, Pastor Teresa!" the children sang out when they were ready for chapel time. They drew pictures to send to shut-ins; everything was picture perfect. I can't say when the earthquake began.

Rumbling. Murmuring. Letters. Phone calls. Dissatisfaction with the director. The Education Committee chair and I conferred several times a week. Disgruntled parents sent out a letter to all the parents. They demanded that the preschool director be fired and accused the pastor, me, of failing to take appropriate action. Now when I stopped at the grocery store, some preschool parents pretended I was an orange in the crate, not a person to be greeted.

"How can you do it?" a friend asked, referring to my calm response to the ugly mass mailing.

"I've faced fire before," I shrugged. "Either people know you or they don't. There's nothing to do but remain positive and stay the course. I can control my own actions and words but not anyone else's actions or words," I told him.

I had worked hard to be the calm presence. The preschool halls, though, felt treacherous. Cutting eyes, suspicious looks, and tension grew like kudzu in the summertime. Some teachers became physically ill due to the tension.

The Church Council began to discuss what to do about the growing attendance and the lack of pew space.

"This is wonderful! We need more space. I think the only option to reaching out to new people is to create a second service," I spoke with enthusiasm.

"But if there were two services it would be like having two congregations and we wouldn't know each other as well. It would divide us," stated one long-time member.

I responded, "If you are determined to know everyone, you will know them."

"What if you leave? You know before you came we had two services, but not enough attendance so we had to combine services," an analytical person asked.

I flushed and blustered. "I am not going anywhere. Even if I did leave, you'd carry on and grow."

The discussion stalemated. I didn't know how to lead them in following the will of God to reach more people. Instead of choosing to grow, they followed their loyalty to the congregation and the safety of remaining unchanged. Sure enough, attendance peaked and then settled. The growth wave had crested.

I was upset with myself. I believed that I had failed. If only I had been a better leader . . . I began to beat myself up.

Thanksgiving drew near; I was looking forward to it. After our foiled Easter vacation, I was chomping at the bit to go to the mountains for a week. I lined up a pastor to be on call. There was less than a week to go before we left on vacation. Ted had been working crazy hours. I was doing school drop-off and pick-up for our daughter, always trying to beat the traffic. Family time was coming—Wahoo!

The call came out of the blue. One day Cynthia's husband, Ray, was making his hair stand up with static electricity in a restaurant to make his grandchildren laugh and embarrass his wife; and the next he was flat on his back in an ambulance. Heart attack.

Cynthia and I met at the hospital. We walked through the double doors into the Intensive Care Unit. In the little cubicle, I stood on one side of the bed while she leaned over him on the other side.

Stroking his cheek she said softy, "Honey, we're here. The preacher's here with me. Teresa's here." His eyelids fluttered.

I called his name and reached for his hand. Cynthia and I talked, trying to include Ray in the conversation. The three of us held hands and prayed, *Dear God, if it is your will, bring healing to this, your child. Watch over Cynthia that she might feel your arms of love. Amen.*

Back in the waiting room, we talked gravely about the situation.

"I'll be back tomorrow. Call if you need me," I said as I left.

I felt for Cynthia. Day after day, I visited the hospital. No change for the better. I knew the policy. After four or five days of no change, the doctors often recommend unplugging the machines—the respirator.

Saturday night my heart ached. I needed this vacation. *Please God,* I prayed, *Please let him hold on until after our vacation.* My tender heart didn't know the word "no" or how to use it.

When I was growing up my dad would say to my mom, "Come and help me, it will only take a minute."

My mother would say, "No, I am in the middle of something." Then she would stop whatever she was doing and go help him. It was never just a minute, or even five or fifteen.

But it was more than that. I thought if I didn't please people they wouldn't love me. I couldn't bear the thought of disappointing them.

When the phone rang on Monday morning I wanted to cry. I couldn't do this funeral. I was exhausted. Still, I answered the phone, "Hello?"

"Teresa, this is Cynthia. There is nothing more they can do. They'll turn the machines off around noon."

I couldn't find the words to say, "I'll call my sub—the pastor on call." All I could think was if it were me, I would want the pastor I knew to be there.

I said, "I'll be there soon." Turning to Ted with tears in my eyes, I wailed. He held me. Then we discussed logistics. Should he wait at the house until I was done at the hospital? We agreed he would.

At the hospital, I woodenly did what I could. I prayed with the family and guided them in saying their goodbyes.

"Your dad can probably hear you. Would you like a moment alone with him?" I sat and waited while each family member took their turn.

Finally, we held hands with dad as he breathed his last. I said a closing prayer.

I was working up the courage to say I needed to go.

Cynthia turned and said, "Teresa, won't you come over to the house with us?" My heart dropped. I smiled a fake smile and said yes. I called Ted; we revised the plan. They would go ahead; I'd drive down later in the day.

Driving down later, I was furious with myself. How could I have done this again? Why couldn't I say what I needed to say? *I'd be honored to conduct his funeral. I'm available next week when I come back from vacation, or if you'd like to have the service sooner I'll contact the pastor on call and she'll conduct the service for you.* Ugh!

I drove down to the mountains on Monday night, then back home on Wednesday for the visitation. After conducting the funeral I drove down again on Thursday afternoon, only to come home on Saturday. Once again I laid down but couldn't rest. I hiked, but was too exhausted to enjoy it or have it to renew me.

ෙෙෙ

When the cold weather arrived the school children didn't go outside. We had assumed that they would do hands-on activities inside if they weren't outside. Wrong! I arrived one day to pick up my girl, only to find the children watching a movie rated PG. Ted and I met with the head of the school.

"We are concerned about the movies the children watch," I began.

"Children are allowed to bring movies from home to watch," the director responded.

Ted asked, "Who checks to make sure they are child appropriate?"

The director had no answer. Day after day the children were told to sit still and watch the movie. Thus, I raced to pick up our daughter before movie time.

ෙෙෙ

Before Christmas, I was falling. No. I'd already fallen. My brain said, "I can't do this" to every task I needed to do. I pushed past my brain's message, but it took everything I had to do it. After work and picking up my girl, I'd get home and upstairs, but no further. I'd lie down on the floor at the top of the stairs. After a while, I'd pull myself together and get dinner together for us.

Ted would come home for dinner, sit on the couch and nod off, then scramble to get back to church for a meeting.

The preschool parent-versus-director conflict went from simmering to boiling over. Finally, all of the church leaders met with the preschool director and me to review the situation. We couldn't find the basis of their complaints. How would we resolve the situation? I drafted a tough response; it was approved. *As parents you have the right to enroll your child and the right to withdrawal your child. You do not have the right to demand staff changes.* With heavy hearts, we asked the concerned parents to meet with us.

"Good afternoon," the meeting began. "Let's introduce ourselves." People were pleasant. We prayed. We turned to the parents, "Please tell us your concerns."

They spoke at length, "We believe the preschool director is a liar." We studied their documents but couldn't find anything except a "he said versus she said" situation. We handed out our statement with regret. Several families withdrew their children from the school.

Christmas came. For the first time all three of us would be at the same midnight service at Ted's church after I had conducted my Christmas Eve services. We hurried into the hushed church. Ted began the service, but I couldn't focus on the words or the music. All I could see was that Ted had gained weight; his suit was too tight. I was embarrassed. When we arrived home, he went to have a sugary snack; I snapped at him irritably. What a way to usher in the birth of Christ.

January plodded on. Evening after evening I fell on the floor at the end of the day. My irritability over simple, stupid things grew.

My child began to bite her fingernails. It was a pet peeve of mine. I barked at her. She cried. I wanted to cry.

I was so tired. I needed support but couldn't find the energy to seek it. I knew I was depressed but didn't want to speak it out loud for fear it would be true.

"Teresa, we need new office equipment. The answering machine isn't working right," Beverly said.

"I'll see what I can do," I responded. After she went home I tried out the answering machine. It worked fine. Her hearing didn't.

The following day I asked, "Beverly, will you go to lunch with me?"

She agreed. We set the date. Driving to the restaurant, I felt butterflies in my stomach.

We ordered our food and I asked, "So how are you doing?"

She spoke of her ailing son. At last, I screwed up my courage. "Beverly, I've checked out the answering machine and it appears to be working correctly."

She looked crestfallen, "I thought I would learn the people's names and do better."

"Beverly, it's your hearing."

"I tried out a hearing aid. It didn't work," Beverly confessed. "I can't afford hearing aids. I spent all of my retirement money on my mentally ill son. He doesn't have insurance."

"I've researched the cost of hearing aids. I can raise the funds," I offered.

"No." She looked horrified.

"I could do it confidentially," I assured her. No. The subject was closed.

In the morning I stopped by her office, "Good morning, Beverly."

She looked at me for a moment; then turned to get something.

"I need to give this to you," she said as she turned back around. Her face was set. I read the letter.

Dear Pastor and Personnel Committee,

I hereby resign as Church Secretary effective Friday . . .

I gasped. "Beverly, this isn't what I want," I protested.

"If I'm not able to do the job, I'm not able to do the job," she said with conviction.

The Personnel Committee was pleased to find that one of the preschool assistants had a gift and calling to be a secretary. Bo was hired immediately.

ॐॐॐ

"Hey, Ted, for my birthday will you spend the afternoon with me?" I was hoping for a romantic afternoon.

"Definitely. One o'clock okay?" he asked.

I dressed up in heels and a skirt on the big day. An hour passed by. I knew what had happened. Someone had stopped by and he'd found it impossible to break away. More time passed before I heard his car, then his footsteps in the hallway.

I looked into his eyes and fell to pieces. I confessed that my depression was back.

"Call the doctor for me, please, make an appointment for me," I begged him. He did as I asked. I wallowed in defeat. How could my brain have done this to me, again?

I saw our general practitioner.

"The last time I felt like this my psychiatrist prescribed twenty milligrams of Prozac a day," I told him.

"Are you seeing a counselor?" he asked. I shook my head, no. "You would probably find that helpful." He then said, "Since I am starting you on this in February and you need to take it at least six months in order to replenish the deficit of serotonin in your brain, you'll have to take this until the spring of 1999. Too many people who are depressed also have Seasonal Affective Disorder, so to take you off in the middle of the winter would be foolish."

I left the office, immensely unhappy. The last time I had taken Prozac I had gained weight. I was angry. Dr. Marnie had told me I might need to take medication for the rest of my life to help my brain function correctly. Why didn't God heal my brain?

Who cared how much I weighed? I decided I did not care.

Slowly, the Prozac lifted me. I no longer fell down on the floor at the top of the stairs. I went up two dress sizes. Months went by and the school sent the children back outside to play. No more racing to pick up my girl. Thank God!

"Ted, did I tell you the good news?" I said to him over the phone in my office. "The renters in my parsonage are moving out. That means we could move to my parsonage."

"I'll check into the situation and let you know," Ted said. When he called back, he had the scoop. "One person in the church told Doug last year that the pastor had to live in their community. It wasn't a church-wide thing. I explained how we've always lived in my parsonages and it was your turn. They're okay with it."

Wahoo! I was dancing with joy. Ted loved to drive; commuting against traffic was fine with him.

November 1999. My daughter's school was less than a mile away. I was a walking woman, walking on air! Ted was up early getting ready for church on Sunday; he jumped into the shower of our "new" parsonage. I heard water flowing. More and more water flowed but it didn't sound like a shower.

"Teresa!" Ted called out. I sleepily went in the bathroom. He stood in the tub with the whole faucet assembly in his hands. The water was pouring out of a pipe in the wall. "You've got to go turn off the water main!"

I ran to turn it off. I laughed about the whole thing, until it was time to tell the trustee whose son was a plumber. I was embarrassed.

"Ted went to take a shower and ended up with the fixture in pieces," I admitted.

He laughed and said he'd get his son to take care of it.

By the time we got home from church, the tub was all back together but I still didn't see how one turned the shower on. There was no knob, lever, or button to be found. Ted came home; we looked it over together. We were mystified.

I called the trustee back. "Ah, this is Teresa. Thanks so much for putting everything back together; but we don't know how to turn on the shower."

He said, "I'll have my son stop by this afternoon."

I thanked him profusely. Later, when the son arrived, we were amazed at the simplicity of the whole thing. The diverter was a ring located on the end of the tub spout. Who would have thought?

My term of taking the Prozac was over. I felt better. I had decided I didn't ever want to talk to my husband and daughter that way again. I didn't want her to grow up like I grew up, fearing irrational fits over small things. I checked out the local counseling website and found a counselor I liked.

"My goal is to have you monitor me. If I start sliding toward the pit, I want you to tell me," I told her. Karla, my new counselor, agreed to watch out for me.

SLAYING THE MONSTER

- Analyze what happened to Teresa that weakened her stability.
- List the stressors prior to Teresa's episode of clinical depression.
- Name the stressors in your life.
- Share with your group what self-care you are doing.

MORE: DEPRESSION PREVENTION INFORMATION

Depression Prevention: Depression can be hereditary and clinical depression can happen without cause. However, there are ways to make becoming depressed less likely.

Self-care is supremely important when trying to prevent depression.

When stress occurs in multiple areas of your life, take care to reduce as much of it as possible. Find ways to share the load at home, at work, and with family and friends.

- Exercise daily
- Get sunlight daily
- Create community
- Develop a support network
- Make time for yourself to simply "be." Depression often comes out of nowhere, sneaking into one's life in slippery small ways

Resources: The book, *Undoing Depression* by Dr. Richard O'Connor, and the blogsite, http://redeemedandsummoned.blogspot.com/2008/05 /bible-verses-for-panic-depression.html

Assurance: God is with you in the darkness (Psalm 88, Isaiah 43).

13

Sunshine, Sea Changes, and Surprises

M Y NEW COUNSELOR, KARLA, had a sense of humor and a warm smile. We clicked. She helped me see that many of the situations I thought were personal, were just situations—not personal at all. It reminded me of what Oprah Winfrey once said. You don't know what's happening, or has happened, to the other person that is causing him or her to treat you the way he or she does.

June was evaluation time for the preschool. With the school year over, the director and I went over teacher evaluations. We'd decided not to offer a new contract to the lone ranger teacher. Within a week a second teacher—a wonderful teacher—told us she would not be returning in the fall. Some of the truth came out. The lone ranger, in an attempt to sabotage the director, had used the second teacher to rile up parents.

Before I knew it August had arrived. It was hard to believe that school would start in three weeks. Ms. Q stopped by my office.

"How are things going?"

"Good," she said. "Enrollment's full. We have a waiting list. I have the teachers I need." She paused uncomfortably. "I have an opportunity to teach at the public school near my house, in the afternoons. I really want to become a public school teacher. What do you think?"

"Afternoons? Hmm. Preschool is over at 12:30 p.m. It wouldn't interfere?" I asked.

She answered quickly, "No. No, I don't think so."

But it wasn't too many days and she was back in my office. "In order for me to take this job—and I really want to take it—I'd have to leave at noon instead of 12:30 p.m.," she said.

"Oh. That's different than leaving after school. I'll have to talk to the Personnel Committee and get back to you," I said with some concern.

The lay leader, Aiden, and the personnel chair, Elmer, and I met.

Aiden's gravelly voice announced, "If Ms. Q leaves before afternoon dismissal we'll need an assistant director; someone who will be responsible for the whole school in her absence."

"If she leaves early, we'll have to reduce her salary to last year's salary in order to fund the assistant director position," added Elmer.

I lined up a meeting; I knew it wasn't going to be pretty. All three of the people meeting with me were strong leaders; all were loathe to back down once a decision had been made.

Elmer laid out the changes necessary to meet Ms. Q's proposal of teaching at the public school.

A storm brewed in Ms. Q's face. "That's not acceptable. If I'm doing the work of director, and I will do *all* of the work, then my salary should remain the same. If the salary is lowered, I will resign," she said. The meeting ended with a stalemate.

The whole Personnel Committee met to review the situation.

Elmer outlined the meeting with Ms. Q, "We're down to the wire. School is to start next week. We don't want to rock the boat or alarm new parents by having the director resign." The committee agreed to her demands with one caveat.

The day was mild, but the meeting wasn't going to be mild. I sat in my office and prayed. Elmer arrived first with a rather grim expression. Aiden followed him in, with warm pleasantries for me, but a somber tone overall.

Ms. Q bustled into the room. She took a seat in the armchair. Her blonde hair shone, while her face reflected stony determination.

"Ms. Q," Elmer began, "It's important to have an assistant director. Deb has agreed to do this job." He paused to draw a breath and perhaps steel himself. "However, the Personnel Committee has decided that if we're to pay you the full salary of director and you'll be leaving at noon instead of the end of the day then, we will place you on probation. Because this is something new, we will review the situation prior to Christmas."

Ms. Q snapped, "If you want me to resign, I'll resign!"

"No," Elmer responded quietly, "We're not asking you to resign. We are simply saying that with this sort of change, we believe it's appropriate to review the situation in November to see if the new arrangements are working well."

Tightlipped, she agreed to the terms and signed her contract. The storm was over; at least, we thought so.

I saw less and less of Ms. Q. No more "drop by my office" chats. On occasion I'd catch her in the hallway and inquire about the school.

"Everything is fine. Just fine," she'd assure me, before moving quickly down the hall. As Thanksgiving drew near, I decided I needed to follow up on Ms. Q's probationary review. Noting the time, I rushed downstairs to catch the teachers before they left for the day.

The playground door bumped shut as the last teacher made her way back into the building following dismissal. I strolled down the hallway with Deb, the assistant director.

She laughed, "You should have seen what John did today in school!" then pointed to the end result of his project.

I didn't waste any time, "When we made the new arrangements with Ms. Q, we agreed to review it by the end of November, to make sure things were running smoothly." The laughter died a quick death. Teachers began to look away. "Do you have any feedback I should take to the Personnel Committee?" I persisted.

Shifting from one foot to the other, in their little circle, one volunteered, "We are concerned—she's been sick. That's made her out of sorts."

"Have you talked with her about it?"

They looked at each other and the teacher answered, "We're afraid to, we don't want her to take our heads off."

"Direct communication is important," I insisted. "I hope you'll find a way to share your concern with her. Is there anything else?" There was nothing. "Let me know if you have other feedback. Have a good afternoon." I headed back down the hall.

When I turned to go upstairs, I was shocked. Every single teacher had followed me.

They began:

"There are days she has to leave earlier than noon, but she isn't telling anyone."

"The Christmas play is coming up. But we haven't had staff meetings, so we teachers went ahead and planned something. When she heard about it, she objected. She had her own ideas. The Christmas play is three weeks away and she hasn't told us what her ideas are."

"The shot records in the children's file folders are incomplete. I offered to help her with them. She turned me down."

"She's never here, and the parents have noticed."

"The Thanksgiving Feast is coming up next week and nothing has been planned or organized. The parents keep asking questions."

"We haven't had our annual fire inspection. Fire drills haven't happened."

"The bathroom fixture is broken, and we asked her to let the Trustees know. She said she already did and they won't fix it."

The color drained from my face. I went home wound up tight. I had backed her and trusted her, but she hadn't asked for help. The Trustees had never been called regarding the bathroom. Our school license was in jeopardy because of the incomplete files. It was all going to come to a head with Christmas. Elmer was out of town for Thanksgiving.

That night, I went back to the church to get the Personnel Policy and study it thoroughly. As the day-to-day supervisor, I did not have firing authority, but I could ask for the director's resignation or put her on a two-week administrative leave.

Morning came. I went in early and posted a note on the director's door. *Please come see me in my office, ASAP. Teresa.*

The minutes ticked by. I heard the teachers come in. I saw the director's car in the parking lot. My secretary arrived. I heard the shouts of children come in the door indicating school had begun. No sign of the director.

I waited another half an hour, unable to focus on anything. Finally, I went down to the preschool. Ms. Q was in her office; my note was still posted in her doorway. I took it off the doorpost.

"Do you have a minute?" I asked. She nodded. In past years, we'd sat in one another's offices brainstorming and sharing. This year had been different. She looked at her desk, then at her computer screen.

"I left a note asking you to come and see me." I held up the post-it.

"I didn't see it," she said too quickly.

"I'm here to ask for your resignation, effective immediately, with two weeks' pay for vacation you have not received," I spoke quickly but couldn't look her in the eye.

"Fine!" she said angrily. "I resign."

I breathed a sigh of relief. "I'll need it in writing by Sunday morning, or I will have to start the process of termination with the Personnel Committee," I added, this time able to face her.

"Why now? Why are you asking me to resign now?" she asked fiercely.

Calmly, I replied, "I think you already know. Please turn in your keys when you leave today. You can fax your resignation in or drop it off, whichever you prefer."

I was shaking inside as I left her office; I'd never asked anyone to resign. To ask her to leave felt like defeat. After she'd left for the day, I met with the teachers and informed them of her resignation.

"She will not be returning after today," I explained. "I'll send a note to the parents on Monday. Is there anything you need from me?" I asked. The teachers' shoulders loosened.

"She was our friend," one teacher remarked wistfully.

The assistant director responded, "We'll be fine. We'll all work together on this." Every teacher nodded in agreement and echoed her conviction.

"The Personnel Committee will meet on Sunday to determine the next step in terms of an interim director."

As people dispersed, I asked the assistant director if I could speak to her for a moment. She nodded.

I asked her, "Are you willing to take the interim director position if the Personnel Committee authorizes it? I believe you are highly qualified and would do an excellent job."

Deb looked me in the eye and said, "I'll do anything to help the school finish out the year. I appreciate the compliment."

I went home and made phone calls to the Personnel Committee.

∽∽∽

The six-month anniversary of when I had begun to meet with Karla, my counselor, came around; we discussed how I was doing.

"Teresa, I believe you have Dysthymia," she said.

"Dysthymia?" I echoed; I'd never heard of it.

"Dysthymia is the medical term used to describe someone who is not clinically depressed but has an ongoing low-grade depression. For instance when a person's clinically depressed it may be impossible to get up and do things; a person with dysthymia can get up and do things but finds change very difficult and stressful. He or she is often irritable without cause. The person doesn't always have the ability to screen what he or she says because the brain is so low on the chemicals that produce energy, good feelings, and balance."

"What does that mean for me?"

Karla paused, "It may mean that you need to take medication for the rest of your life, in order to live life to the fullest."

I sat in stony silence. A tear rolled down my cheek, then another one. I was awash on a sea of betrayal. *God, how could you have made me so broken and limited? How could my body betray me like this? It's bad enough I've gained fifty pounds since going on Prozac almost two years ago.* Now a second person was telling me the same thing.

I heaved a big sigh. "Are there alternatives to medication?" I asked. We continued to talk. I vowed to find the answer for me. I left Karla's office and drove straight to the library. In the mental health section, I picked out book after book. I staggered to the check out carrying *Prozac Free, Thin for Life,* and more.

∾ ∾ ∾

That Christmas all seemed right with the world, at least in our little family. We built gingerbread houses on Christmas Day and went to see friends.

I journaled about the dysthymia and my weight.

> *December 28, 1999. I vow to lose weight in the coming year; I'll read every book I can find on weight loss.* Prozac Free *talks about exercise and diet, it talks about self-care and homeopathic physicians. It can't hurt to check it out. The National Homeopathic Organization is in Alexandria, Virginia.*
>
> Prozac Free *was right—there are a lot of different kinds of people claiming to be homeopathic in one way or another.* Prozac Free *encourages you to find one trained classically. I find two. One doesn't return my phone calls. The second says we can do it over the phone after I fill out a long form.*

"What?" I asked the homeopathic doctor to repeat herself.

"Usually, I have a person fill out a detailed report and then mail it to me. I examine the report and talk with you on the phone. I tell you what I think would make a difference for you," said the doctor who studied in Britain and was from India.

I was aghast! She thought she could diagnose me over the telephone? I balked.

"I'd prefer to come and see you," I persisted.

She paused at length, "All right. Let's set up an appointment."

I filled out the questionnaire, pages in length. It asked unusual questions like: Do you often feel cold? What position do you normally sleep in? Fetal? On your back? On your side?

I drove an hour north to meet her. I told her all about trying to lose weight. She prescribed for me a number of homeopathic remedies. I shared with her my struggle with depression and dysthymia. She wrote out her recommendations.

At the end of the conversation she added, "When allergy season comes around take Sabbadilla 30c and that should do the trick for you."

She had given me hope. I started taking the remedies she had prescribed. Then I received her letter with a detailed nutritional and exercise guideline sheet to follow. According to the paper, food allergies sometimes caused depression. I was determined to try everything before I gave in to medication.

I stopped eating white flour, white sugar, beef, and chocolate. I was to have less than four hundred milligrams of salt a day and no foods that were processed or had preservatives. There was nothing left to eat, I thought sadly. Also eucalyptus, garlic, and mint counteracted the effect of the remedies so I had to avoid them.

Back to the library I went, this time I was searching for recipes. I began to eat a non-fat, carrot soup for lunch most days. I found some old VCR tapes of Jane Fonda's workouts in the thrift store.

Every day after I picked my daughter up from school I went to the basement and sweated with Jane Fonda for an hour and a half. I ate a plain sweet potato for supper. I had peas for a snack or sometimes home-popped popcorn. I lost weight steadily. I liked that.

April 2000. After four months of homeopathic remedies my body felt good, but my brain was unchanged. I went to my regular appointment with Karla.

"Okay, I give up. Give me the name of the psychiatrist," I said.

I made the appointment with Dr. Oh and was soon in her office. Files were stacked and heaped along the wall. I told her my life story, explained my experience with Prozac and my tendency to gain weight. I was pleased with how well she listened.

"In the old days, we would medicate people only when they were in the midst of an episode of clinical depression; but nowadays we believe it is more effective to have someone take medication continuously and prevent the rollercoaster of depression," Dr. Oh said. I slumped on the couch, feeling defeated and angry with my brain for being so inadequate.

Dr. Oh went on, "There is one new medication that has a side effect of weight loss instead of weight gain. Would you like to try that?" I nodded.

She gave me a sample and said, "Come back and see me in two weeks."

When our day off arrived, Ted and I headed to the park. The green hills rolled beside the gentle waves of the Potomac River. We walked and walked before I found the words.

"I am now under the umbrella of *mental illness*," I said angrily. Ted let me rage.

"I do *not* want to be mentally ill! I do not want to take medication for the rest of my life! Why can't they call it broken brain syndrome? Why can't we acknowledge that it is no different than other broken things like a broken leg?"

When I quieted down, Ted said, "Taking antidepressants is no different than someone taking medication for diabetes for the rest of their life."

"I disagree! Diabetes isn't under the umbrella of mental illness. It's considered physical. At least diabetics aren't considered dangerous and crazy!" I retorted.

Two weeks later, I was meeting with Dr. Oh. "I think the shakiness has almost gone away," I reported.

"Good. Come back in four weeks," she said.

Four weeks flew by. I grumbled to myself as I tried to make up time driving to my appointment. I'd left the office late. As I wheeled into a parking space, I was still disgusted that I had to keep coming back to see the psychiatrist so often.

Dr. Oh greeted me pleasantly, "How's the dry mouth?"

"It's a little better," I ventured.

"How's the energy level?" she inquired.

I stopped for a moment. "It's . . . it's a lot better." I hadn't even paid attention to my newfound energy.

~ ~ ~

Summertime had arrived and we were off to the mountains in West Virginia. Ted had rented a cabin for us. I was really grumpy although I didn't know why.

I went for long hikes on top of the mountain ridges. I moved like a mountain goat along the switchbacks and ridges. I was angry. I tried to push the anger away, push it out and up to God in prayer. I wished for a husband who was an extrovert.

The three of us went hiking in the afternoon but it was sticky, slow and unsatisfying. Ted stopped to visit with a guy in the rec room. My girl and I took to the swings. Soon, it was naptime for our girl, so we returned to the cabin.

"Play a game with me," I said to Ted. I got out the game board.

"I'll play if I get to go first," Ted remarked as he sat down.

I exploded. "*What?*" I roared. "You can't even play a game with me without saying you won't do it, unless you get to go first?!"

Ted said nothing.

"I can't believe you," I yelled. "I have to ask for time and conversation!" He sat very still. I looked around the cabin wildly. "That's it," I said with finality. "*I'm leaving.*"

Then as I stomped out the door I tossed the words over my shoulder, "I'm never coming back." I got in the car and drove off. As I did, I glimpsed my four-year-old standing at the door with Ted.

Tears flooded my face and horror flooded my mind—my daughter just heard and saw me say I was never coming back. I yelled at God. I screamed in the car. I drove the winding roads not knowing where I was or what I should do. I drove and drove, weeping and gnashing my teeth.

The sun was sinking. I stopped for ice cream, but in a fit of anger threw it away. I thought about renting a hotel room; that would show Ted I was serious! Then I remembered Helen at the door . . . my heart was shredded by the memory. I walked across the street to a drugstore and bought a stuffed horse for my girl and a card for Ted. My tail was between my legs.

I forced myself to drive back to the cabin. Numbed. Soaked with tears. Regret drove the car.

As soon as I pulled up, Helen ran out to meet me. I picked her up. She was already in her pajamas; I got in bed with her and sang her to sleep.

Ted was in bed with his back turned toward me. Our exchange of words wasn't a discussion. It was ultimatums, first by me, then by him. They did not match. I cried myself to sleep.

The next day we drove home. I felt nothing but pain. Ted and I were together but estranged. I left the two of them at the house. Driving down the familiar street, I thought, *It hasn't been this bad since the first year when we were married and I was so deeply depressed . . .* That was it! I pulled over rapidly. With cell phone in hand, I dialed Dr. Oh's emergency number.

Her answering machine kicked in, "You have reached Dr. Oh. If this is a life-threatening emergency please hang up and dial 911. If you are in need of a call back, Dr. Neer is on call for me. Please call him at the following number . . . *beep.*" Breathless, I called the number.

"Hello, this is Dr. Neer's answering service, how may I help you?"

"I'm Dr. Oh's patient and her machine said Dr. Neer's on call for her. I need to talk to him as soon as possible."

I sat and waited for him to call me back on my cell phone.

"Hello?"

"Hello, is this Teresa Smith?" Dr. Neer asked.

"Yes."

"How may I help you?" his kind voice floated to my ear.

Tears washed the words back and forth, before I could speak, "I . . . I . . . I . . . am on Welbutrin and have taken it for six weeks. All of a sudden it feels like the bottom has dropped out on me. I went away for the week and was off the charts with anger and irritability over stupid things."

"That happens. Sometimes after six weeks, you need an increase in the dosage. Give me your pharmacy number and I will call it in for you," he said.

"Thank you," I said gratefully.

Medication: got to get it and take it. Got to pick up the pieces of my marriage. Within a week, the new dosage had me positively flying. I handled change easily and thought, *Is this how it is for regular people? Little stupid things happen and they laugh?*

I laughed about a broken dish. Whoa! I'd waited all of my life to feel like other people. My days were neutral now, not everything was challengingly difficult. Ordinary tasks were, well, ordinary.

I kept meeting with Karla. It'd become clear. I didn't believe in myself. When I'd been depressed, I couldn't have spotted this self-worth thing if it had been nine feet tall and in my face.

I asked her, "Self-worth, self-esteem. Is it a computer chip you can just slip in?"

She smiled and laughed. Then sobering up she said, "No, it's a total rewiring job."

I wanted to fold up right there.

"More work!" I exclaimed. "How can it be I get one thing 'fixed' and then more stuff comes to the front of the line?"

We talked, laughed, and planned.

I kept up my weight loss and exercise routine. I had less than fifteen pounds to lose. Now that I had energy I began to evaluate my work as a pastor. I concluded I needed a sabbatical. I was dried up. Our denomination allowed for a sabbatical. You just had to educate your Personnel Committee, find funding, get the superintendent's and bishop's approvals, and more.

I was well, but not that well. The idea of trying to educate my Personnel Committee seemed impossible. I dreamed of taking a sabbatical but didn't even think of planning it. The dream died.

I was bored. Spiritually I was a husk. Preach? How? I'd said all I knew to say and found myself distant from God.

Vacation Bible School interrupted my reflections. Children and teachers streamed in. Children who had entered middle school became helpers in the younger children's classes.

One father got stressed over the worship service for homeless people happening at the same time as Vacation Bible School. Somehow homeless people were more dangerous than the rest of us.

Another parent was upset, "I can't believe it; the air quality out there is horrible. Why in the world did the VBS director have the kids go outside for story time?"

I made eye contact, listened, then said, "We can talk to her, I'm sure she was thinking about Jesus teaching on the hillside."

After the children left on the third day, the director approached me about a middle schooler.

"Teresa, it's Jane. She put a child in a headlock on the playground!"

I smiled a little. Jane had managed to behave for three days; that was pretty amazing!

"Have we talked to the parents of the child Jane put in a headlock about the incident?" I inquired. We made plans to do so. "Now, about tomorrow, I'll keep Jane with me." I looked forward to spending time with her. For five years I had watched this child grow. She was delightful, hyperactive, and lived with a guardian, not her own parent who had many issues. She came to church alone and often walked out during the sermon. Through the window I'd seen her take branches and whack trees while I preached. I wondered if I had ever prayed harder for anyone else.

The next evening started with another child teasing her, "Jane, Jane, you are a big pain!" Jane tried to get the boy. I caught up with the two of them.

"Come on, let's go outside. Tell me what's going on."

Jane was red in the face and angry, "He made fun of me! He's always teasing me."

Her friend looked sheepish.

"Do you two like being teased?"

"No," shouted Jane. Her friend shook his head and examined an ant on the sidewalk.

"Does it matter what other people say about you?"

We discussed the situation thoroughly and the two went their separate ways but not before I called out, "Hey, Jane, you get to spend the evening with me."

She didn't ask why. She came along willingly and helped me with the simple tasks I had. In between story sessions, we hung out in my office.

Gently I asked, "Do you know why you are here with me tonight?"

She refused to answer. She looked out the window at the chokecherry tree.

"Jane, sometimes when bad things happen to us or are said to us, we begin to believe them. Sometimes, they become a recording in our brain. Then when someone teases us the recording switches on and says the teaser is right—we aren't worth anything. But do you know what?"

She looked at me reluctantly, "What?"

"You can make a new tape recording for yourself! There are only two people whose opinions count. One is God. God says, 'You are my cherished child. I love you, Jane. I love you more than life itself. I want the best for you.' Can you guess who the other person is?"

Jane shrugged and tugged at her shoe.

"You! Your opinion is the other one. If your brain is telling you that you don't matter or something else negative, you can change the recording."

She looked interested but at the same time I could read her thoughts, *Lady, you are crazy.*

"Your brain is really powerful. But you have power over your brain. You get to choose the messages it gives you. The message God wants you to have in your brain is that you are loved, worth a whole lot."

"Sure," Jane mumbled, "yeah right. Like I could change the message."

"Do you want to know how to change the message?" I asked her. "Want to know how to make a new recording for yourself?" I was eager to share the secret. I was praying hard that she'd be able to hear this.

"You say it to yourself over and over again while you look in the mirror, 'I am a cherished child of God.' Every time you say it, it records a little bit of the message in your brain. It tapes over some of the bad stuff. When the bad stuff starts playing you say, "Nope, I am a cherished child of God."

Jane looked a little interested, but mostly skeptical.

"If you do this over and over every day for the whole summer, it won't matter who calls you what, because you will be confident and know in your brain and your heart who you are—a cherished child of God."

"You're sure about that, huh?" she asked.

"Yes, I am." I glanced at the clock and realized we were needed on the playground.

With Vacation Bible School over and the summer stretched out ahead of me, I felt dry. Thirteen years in ministry and I was in a drought-stricken land. Bone dry. The fact that the church had balked at my leadership about a second service still haunted me. I was searching for water.

A brochure fell into my hands about doctor of ministry degree programs. The brochure said there were a number of tracks to choose from. I thought about it. I really needed to bone up on Evangelism (one possible track), but I felt called to the track of Story and Spirituality; it would feed my soul. I entered into a time of deep prayer and tug of war on the subject. I talked to my Personnel Committee about returning to school and the amount of time I would be away from the congregation to complete the degree. Then I applied for the Story and Spirituality program.

∾∾∾

At Christmas I reached my goal of 148 pounds! I was thrilled. I had been accepted into the DMIN program of my choice. Our five-year-old was happy at school. Ted was excited about ministry. Our marriage felt strong and right. Upon entering the program in May of 2001, I knew I'd been sent to the right place. It brought springtime to my soul.

SLAYING THE MONSTER

- Reflect on the term "mental illness" and your understanding of it, as well as society's myths.
- Have you ever heard of dysthymia? How did it affect Teresa?
- Consider the conversation about self-esteem Teresa had with Jane. What are the tape recordings from your childhood that your brain plays?
- Choose a verse from the Bible that describes God's love for you. Memorize it this week.

MORE: DYSTHYMIA AND SELF-ESTEEM INFORMATION

Dysthymia: The American Psychiatric Association defines dysthymia as depressed mood most of the time for at least two years, along with at least two of the following symptoms: poor appetite or overeating; insomnia or excessive sleep; low energy or fatigue; low self-esteem; poor concentration or indecisiveness; and hopelessness. (www .healthharvard.edu)

Self-esteem: Many who suffer from depression also suffer from a lack of self-esteem. Self-esteem—believing oneself is loved, lovable, and worthwhile—develops over time with continual affirmation. A child will develop healthy self-esteem when praised appropriately.

Assurance: We love because God first loved us (Matthew 10:30–31, Psalm 139, 1 John 4:11). Resource: http://www.equippedforliving .org/pdfs/destructive/Chapter%202.pdf

14

Suffering Reborn

DAYS BEFORE I ATTENDED the mandatory Sexual Ethics Training event required by the Virginia Annual Conference, I had dreams—bad dreams. Dreams of a person and a situation I thought I'd left behind twenty years before.

The day came, a regular mild day. But getting out of my car in the parking lot felt treacherous. I started toward the church when a fellow clergyman got out of his car nearby. The first words out of his mouth startled, then angered, me.

"Instead of attending this event we ought to just have sex in the parking lot," he casually remarked. I didn't know the guy, so quickly walked toward the building without commenting.

The fellowship hall was extremely crowded. I sought out friends and we sat down at a table near the back door. There I was with Ted and Gary, when others sat down. Directly across from me sat down a clergyman who was a predator—a sexual predator. Victims had confessed to one of my longtime friends but never could bring themselves to file formal charges. I was in knots.

The presentation began. They spoke of the high percentages of women who have been sexually harassed, abused, or assaulted; my clergywomen friends and I exchanged sad knowing looks—we had shared many of our personal experiences with one another over the years. The morning wore on. Around lunchtime a film by Marie Fortune was shown. It graphically illustrated what happened when a clergyman became a sexual predator, preying on staff and congregants alike. As the film concluded it illustrated how difficult it was for victims to come forward and bring charges, let alone make them stick.

I was suddenly nineteen years old again—a college student being sexually abused by my youth pastor. I fled the room as if someone were chasing me.

"The sanctuary," was my first thought, "go to the sanctuary."

In the sanctuary a number of senior pastors were talking loudly on cell phones. Rapidly, I left the building. Around the corner, I found some unused steps. There I sat, sobbing, flooded by my past and deep sadness. Shakily, I called Karla to schedule an appointment. I wanted to run away, go as far away as I could—but I knew I couldn't escape the past.

Collecting myself, I marched up to the registrar of the event.

"Is there a place provided for me? Are there people waiting to help folks like me who had flashbacks of abuse?"

The registrar shook his head no.

"Are there people waiting to help predators come to terms with their actions?"

Again the answer was no. Nothing.

The training was mandatory. I made myself re-enter the room. But I couldn't sit still. I tried to sit in the hallway but the memories continued to assault me. I left early. Drove around. Finally went home.

In one swift afternoon, springtime was gone and it was winter in my soul. For more than a year I'd been puzzling over Julie and Eugene's grief and shaken beliefs. When their son had been murdered, I'd watched as their faith in God shattered. The pieces had been too small to pick up. Now in the winter of my soul, I understood.

First, I called it a faith-quake. It all seemed so sudden and carried with it such immediate devastation. The aftershocks kept coming.

Then it was as if I had saved up every bit of anger for my thirty-eight years, and the faith-quake broke it open. I'd never been angry with God. I'd always believed in a loving God. God didn't cause my father to be physically and verbally abusive or shape him into a man that no one could ever please. God didn't cause my mother to submit to this abuse year after year. God didn't place me in the situation that found me depressed and vulnerable to the predator youth pastor.

As I grieved the loss of protection, the lack of unconditional love, and the violation of my soul, I entered into the very *pit* of darkness. Doubt surrounded me. I fought to keep my head above water in a sea of angry, unending waves.

∾∾∾

The doctor of ministry program didn't pause for personal situations, and I'd been taught to pull myself up by my own bootstraps, to ignore pain. So in January I drove through a gentle snowfall to Nashville for two required courses. There our autobiographical papers were returned to us from a previous semester.

Gnashing of teeth rose up in the room as the papers were distributed. Cries of unfairness: classmates felt crushed that they had shared their personal story and been graded with something less than an A. Perspective was lost as to what the assignment had been—compare and contrast a portion of your spiritual autobiography with those of the autobiographies we had read in class.

I received an A but felt chagrined for my fellow students. Sitting next to me, a sister clergywoman had received an A as well. I asked her if I could read her paper.

She said, "Sure."

In her I found a guide. She, too, had suffered at the hands of her parents. She, too, had been sexually abused. She was wise beyond her years. She listened to me.

The first course was "Life Story and Spiritual Practices." Mid-week we were assigned the task of writing a Psalm. I stomped about campus. I did *not* want to be introspective. I did *not* feel contemplative. I had nothing good to say to God and wasn't that what the Psalms were about? With the deadline approaching, I threw myself down sideways in a chair and spilled my soul:

PSALM OF SUFFERING—MY ANGUISH

I am wounded, Creator of the Universe!
What were you thinking?
Why did you allow pain?
Create it?
Will it?
I wrap myself tight against you
and your wound-inflicting, gut-wrenching, stench-producing,
filthy, offending world.
I try to wash out the lingering evil smell and scabs.
I have rolled it up in the car trunk—
stomped on it in the bathtub—

smashing and swirling it in deep water—
trying to wash out the woundedness.
My back aches, my belly throbs, my teeth wear away from grinding.
Still the TV assaults me with breaking glass, naked flesh, echoing
gunfire, burning buildings, falling people, bombing reports, "collat-
eral damages," and burning words.

I thought you were a God of beauty and grace, honor and love,
healing and art.

Instead I am repelled by this broken world,
crushed by this ongoing violence, afflicted by disease.
I ache.
You sit in the corner.
I mop up blood—the blood of creation.
You sit in silence.
I cry and weep until the tears seep into my ears and nose.
You watch stone-faced.
I did not create this mess—why should I clean it up?

You gave my father speech and his words wounded me.
You gave my mother strength that she did not use.
You placed me in a fearful place and did not lend me your arm.
You gave my pastor/mentor skill and he violated my core being.
You are a God of Power and I needed Your Power.
You set me into being in a time of crisis and conflict.
You reared me in a world where the truth was experienced but
never told.
You set examples before me of powerlessness and raging harm.

You! I wrap my arms tight against you and your kind.
You! How can you heal one and not another?!
You! Starve whole nations by withholding rain!
You allow hate to grow, evil to flourish, airplanes to be smashed!
You call me to submit.
I was submitted my whole childhood
to work and relentless impossible standards.
You surround me on every trip home with a blood bath
active wounds weeping, open mouths talking, but not
communicating.

You provide healing and I question it!
You create peace and I cry it is not enough!
You bring solutions and I say,
"Why did I have to have the disease that needed a solution?"
You provide chairs and I say they are too hard.
You give me teachers and I am too self-absorbed to hear.
You place me in streams of life-giving water and I say, "It is too
late."

I am wounded, bleeding, alone, surrounded by wounds and
blood,
pus and static, knives and demands.
You call me to love you,
to be healed
to be transformed
to be.

I say, "I am angry!" and you say,
"Yes, I created that."
I say, "Look! I am bleeding," and you say,
"Ah, see how it washes out the wound
and carries platelets to the surface to begin the mending?"
I say, "How could you immerse me in such pain?" and you say,
"Yes, I made you with a full range of feelings."

I say, "Do you hear me?
I am sick to death of grief and politeness, of pain and kindness,
of mentoring and waywardness, of predators and . . ."

You interrupt and say, "Yes, you are made in my image
and sometimes I too am sick to death of grief and politeness, of
pain and kindness, of mentoring and waywardness,
of predators and . . ."
Amen.

࿎ ࿎ ࿎

That evening Ted called.

"Teresa, I got a call from Lois Johnston. She said her husband died."
Time stood still. I had expected Jay's death, yearned for him to be released
from his physical condition, but I loved him.

"Will you go and visit her?" I asked Ted. He agreed to do so. I pictured him driving his SUV up the steep driveway to the house that looked

like a cottage in a fairytale. Wisteria thicker than my leg wound its way around the screen porch in back. Everyone was a back-door guest walking through a porch, like my grandparents had had on their house.

You went through the galley kitchen crammed with good things and arrived in the living room that had an enormous stone fireplace made by Jay himself. Some salesman once told Jay and Lois that their fireplace was fit for a mansion, not their little shack. They had laughed.

Ted called me back later, "She's doing all right. She was relieved that her Jay was at peace. She's looking forward to you being back in town for the funeral next week."

Slowly, I worked up the courage and asked my classmate, "How did you make peace with the sexual abuse?"

"I did years of therapy, some memory work, and then I went to my parents' home and confronted them," she said. She told me about their reaction, or rather their non-reaction.

"My abuser was not a family member," I said. "He was my youth pastor. How do I . . . what do I do to make sure others aren't victimized like I was?" I asked her.

Over lunch she explained their Conference process and told me whose office to call. Immediately, I picked up the phone. I reached an answering service.

With dragging footsteps and racing heart I returned to class. The instructor's muted purple sweater was like her voice, muted and distant. I doodled. I wondered if I could follow through.

"Take a fifteen minute break and we'll meet back at three," the instructor's voice broke through my battling thoughts. I leapt up like a hurdler at the sound of the start gun, found a quiet place, and dialed the number again.

"This is J.A.'s office. How may I help you?" The voice was strong and steady.

"Yes. I called earlier. I'm an ordained elder serving in the Virginia Conference of the United Methodist Church. I'm trying to follow up on a youth pastor who sexually abused me in 1983. I'm pretty sure I wasn't the only victim. I want to know if he's ever been charged or tried."

"Was he ordained in our conference?" she asked.

"No, he was a lay pastor," I answered.

"Then if he had been charged or convicted, you'd have to check the criminal court records. I'm scrolling through them right now. No. There's no record of him being charged. The best way to proceed is to write a letter of documentation to the bishop and then I'll investigate the matter, to see if he was ever brought up on charges within the church."

I was late for class. Slinking into a back seat, I tried, really tried, to pay attention, but it was like my pen had a mind of its own. It raced across the pages of my notebook.

The minute class was dismissed I charged up to my room and plugged in my computer. The keys clicked rapidly and words filled the screen. Saving the document, I headed out to a class reception. On the way I called Ted.

"I did it. I called the Conference office. There's no criminal record though."

"Wow. That was fast. Now what?" he asked.

"Write a letter of documentation is what they said. I've rewritten it twice already. I have to send it to the Wisconsin bishop and then the conference will investigate. Oh. I'm here now at the reception. I gotta go."

"Love you. Bye!"

After supper, I worked briefly on a paper for class. One more day of class. I hoped to have my friend read my letter of complaint and help me make it sound clear and appropriate. Then the minute I got home to Virginia, I'd fill in the blanks on the dates and send it off.

I felt giddy. I was filled with dread. It was exciting to finally have a way to pursue and maybe prevent it from happening to anyone else in the UMC! I felt bad that it had taken me eighteen years to speak up. Hans could be retired by now, but I didn't think so. My friend thought that he may have already been charged and prosecuted—there had been many rumors about him.

I journaled and journaled:

> *O Divine One, El Shaddai, I lay this in your hands and lay my head on your breast. Stroke my hair, relax my gut, release me from this weight of terror of finally doing something. Allow me to rest in your arms. Amen.*

I opened my Bible to read before sleep and it fell open to Isaiah, chapter forty. "Comfort O comfort, speak tenderly . . . she has served her term . . . lift up your voice with strength—do not fear. El Shaddai will gather the lambs to her bosom."

It was happening in waves now. Last night I went to a worship service with candlelight, stringed instruments, and beautiful voices singing
in Latin. I cried with my forehead resting on the pew in front of me; my
tears fell on the stone floor. I wept over the past, the pastor who loved me
and mentored me. I sobbed for the years that I'd spent bound by this pred-
atory behavior of his. The secret had been a stone I'd carried for decades. I
shed tears for what I was about to do, tears for how flawed a human being
Hans is and was, and tears for the years I couldn't speak truth.

There had been decades of time, when I—truthteller woman—
couldn't tell my family the truth. Oh, I told the story anonymously in the
Virginia Conference *Advocate*. I told the story to my clergy sisters, to my
counselor, and to Ted before we were married. This sharing of my life
story, no doubt saved my life. Yet still the stone was heavy. I hadn't told
the authorities who might have done something. I hadn't told Hans the
consequences I'd borne all these years.

That night in bed, the years between now and then disappeared. Hans's
face was before me. The way Hans used me flowed over me. I pushed and
pushed mentally to remove him. Delete him. Erase him. I tried to insert
my beloved Ted into my thoughts and visions. The battle was hard and I
was losing. Turning on the lamp, I opened my Bible. The Song of Solomon
appeared. Its tenderness and beauty filled me with the sweet and tender
mutualness of making love with Ted. The Scripture helped realign my
thoughts. I relaxed some.

At seven o'clock I was suddenly awake, wide awake. I had been
dreaming of machine guns and children, bombs and barnyards, moving
homes, silos, and holding a child's hands—that were not the hands of my
own child. My conclusion: I was wrapped around the axle.

Jerking open my journal I wrote out my screams. I screamed at
God,

> *Why did you let this happen to me? Why did I have to suffer and*
> *spend so long in pain and take so long to get to wholeness?! Images*
> *of Mom throwing a pitch fork at Dad—really towards him. Her aim*
> *was as good as mine—lousy. We were sorting cattle. He's yelling and*
> *blaming her for steers that were running past him. He picked up the*
> *pitch fork covered in manure and hurled it. It pierced the back of her*
> *thigh and stuck there.*

I screamed at God in an exhausted mental voice. Why did I have to see this stuff again and again in my head? It made me want to write more letters to Dad. Painful, brutally honest letters like I hadn't written in years.

It was seven-thirty a.m. I was so taut you could have bounced a quarter off of my belly. We were driving the twelve hours home today. I needed to be well rested. I was well nightmared instead. Tears leaked out. My gut ached. My hand wrote. The birds sang.

Then I saw snow and winter surrounded me. I was immersed in calmness, feeling crisp and alive. The stars were bright. The ice was smooth and for a moment I was glad to be alive. Imagine that? Glad to be alive.

∾∾∾

Home again, jiggity jig, at midnight to an eager husband. Saturday found me surrounded by old journals in a fog of memories. I searched the pages to verify the sexual abuse. If brains could be wound up tight like overwound springs—my brain would be sprung with anxiety. With Ted's help, I searched my heart. What did I need for peace? I made an appointment with Karla.

I sent the letter to the bishop of Hans's conference:

Dear Bishop,

In November the Virginia Conference had mandatory sexual ethics training for all clergy. When I attended the session, it caused me to flashback to 1983 and re-enter counseling. I have been aware of the abuse since it occurred but have only now found my voice to address it publicly.

I gave in-depth details and concluded:

I have had no contact with Hans over the last twelve years. After I moved out, another vulnerable woman was invited to live in his home. I had always thought it odd that another woman had lived there prior to 1983 but she had left her furniture, moved to California, and had no contact with the family. I now see a clear pattern and have every reason to believe he continues to prey on young vulnerable women. I write that others might be protected. I am willing to provide further details if needed. Thank you for your time and attention to this matter. You may contact me at my home.

Monday morning I worked on Jay's funeral preparations. Tuesday I conducted the funeral, and in the evening I visited a family who had battled Parkinson's disease for twelve years. Wednesday found me at chapel with the preschoolers. After chapel I went home to bed. No energy. Sore throat. Earache. Headache. I handed off materials for the evening meeting I was supposed to attend. Thursday I stumbled into the office to finish prep for Sunday. No talking. Talking hurt. I saw Karla, who helped me deal with the whiplash of fear and vulnerability from the letter I had written. I showed her the Psalm I had written.

"Wow!" she said.

I smiled and said, "I'm a great writer."

She said, "Yes" then asked, "Can I keep this?"

I was flattered. She added, "There's ten sessions worth in this alone."

I was no longer flattered. Back to bed.

Friday, two hours of being out of bed totally wore me out. Talking hurt. I was supposed to co-lead a retreat that night and the next day. I called the co-leader. My voice was so deep and hoarse he thought he was talking to Ted. Ted said he'd preach for me on Sunday, but only if I didn't go to all of the retreat. I couldn't believe I was so sick!

I decided to go to the Friday night part of the retreat but not the Saturday part. By three o'clock the illness crushed the decision. I called the co-leader with the news.

He said, "We'll cancel the retreat."

"No," I objected.

He said, "Okay." I went back to bed. Five minutes later he called back. "You sound like you should go to bed. I'll handle the retreat."

"I won't argue with you," I confessed. I lay down. In all my years of ministry I'd never missed a Sunday due to illness! I missed being in church.

Tuesday I went into the office. After two hours the staff looked at me, the small lunch group looked at me, they all told me to go home to bed. Was I that sick? I wobbled home and lay down.

The Olympics were on TV. Those snowboarders and downhill skiers were crazy! That night there was a figure skater skating on a broken foot. This was glorified and admired. Talk about sick behavior! Abuse your body and we will applaud. Wait, isn't that what I grew up with and wasn't that what I was doing by going to work sick?

Thursday—back with Karla.

"I'm really angry," I told her.

She nodded, "Your psalm reflects that."

"I've never been angry with God before. How can this be?"

"You can't be angry with someone you don't trust," she responded.

Was this true, I wondered? Was it true I had not really trusted God in the past?

January turned into May and still winter laid heavy upon my soul. The next set of courses started; we were studying African American Novels as Theological Source of Spirituality. I found myself in the book *Beloved*, by Toni Morrison. No. I'd never endured what the now-freed grandmother called "Baby Suggs" had endured.

Baby Suggs had endured slavery, the selling of her children, and leaving her remaining family to be free. But somehow the love of God flowed through her and shone in her as she preached in the clearing of her new community to other freed slaves. She was a spiritual leader. She led the freed slaves in learning love and community, hope and delight in one another and God.

Then came the enormous celebration. Her daughter-in-law had run away from the slaveholder and came straight to Baby Suggs. Baby Suggs was reunited with her grandchildren. Family! She threw an enormous party. The next day the after-party glow dimmed the community's alertness to danger.

Baby Suggs was in the garden when she smelled it. Danger. Fear. No one had seen it coming. The slave hunters had pulled up in front of her house. Swift as lightning, her daughter-in-law rushed the grandchildren to the wood shed. The slave hunters found the escaped slave, Baby's daughter-in-law, in the woodshed trying to murder her children. She was trying to save them from a fate worse than death—slavery.

The daughter-in-law was carted off to jail. Baby Suggs took to her bed, her faith shattered. Baby Suggs spent the rest of her days studying the faded brown colors in her bedroom.

What happened? How could a strong woman, a woman who had survived enormous evil and heartbreak, go from leading the community and shining the light, to being broken and bedfast? I could identify with her suffering, with her empowerment and deep faith, and with her crash of faith. I dug deeply into her character. What was it that she was not taught that allowed this crack in her foundation of faith?

I searched history books for clues of what happened on slave plantations. What were the slaves taught? Who taught them? The white preachers taught the slave communities about sin and the love of Jesus, about heaven and forgiveness by God. They left out the parts about Jesus setting the captives free. They emphasized Paul's words telling slaves to be true to their masters.

It was a lack of Christology that Baby Suggs suffered. The white preachers intentionally omitted the message of the power of the risen Christ, the cry of liberation, when preaching to slaves. Baby Suggs's foundation lacked a theology of suffering that embraced Jesus who saved us here on earth and in heaven. Her foundation lacked Jesus's cry for justice and mercy. Her theology of suffering did not go beyond the fact that suffering was to be endured because "the chariot will swing low and carry me home" some day.

Aha! The congregation and I were missing the same two things. First, we were missing a heart knowledge of the suffering of Jesus Christ and the suffering of God. We had the head knowledge down pat, but it wasn't strong enough to build a faith foundation upon. Second, we were missing a theology of suffering. We had chosen to pretend suffering didn't exist in our personal lives in any meaningful way. We yearned to believe that God didn't have anything at all to do with suffering. At the center of a strong theology of suffering was a strong understanding of Jesus and his suffering: Christology.

Baby Suggs took to studying the colors of her bedroom. With my aha moment in hand, I took to studying God and anger. I searched the bookshelves and questioned colleagues. My friends backed away from me when I spoke about being angry with God. Sorting it through with Karla took time. A lot of time. Finally I was ready. I recorded it in my journal for posterity:

> June 24, 2002. Before we left on vacation I wrote three letters: one to my bishop, one to the Board of Ministry Chair, and one to the Sexual Ethics Response Team. Each letter asked for Sexual Ethics Training to be revised and for folks to develop follow-up for those in need of a second step. I included my personal story. Ted helped me craft the letters so they were sharp. I have given permission for them to be shared with everyone deemed necessary. Gulp. I sent them on Friday. Went into crisis mode, feeling vulnerable.

ᐩᐩᐩ

January 2003. A full year later, having sorted through what it means to be sexually abused, I wrote a letter to the perpetrator. I invited him to carry the suffering; I would no longer keep silent. It felt good to be free of the silence and fear. Speaking it aloud changed everything for me.

SLAYING THE MONSTER

- When we believe we are powerless, we bury things deep within ourselves. When and how did Teresa do this? When and how have you done this?

- We have the power to address whatever we choose to address. What did Teresa do to claim power in this chapter?

- Share a time when you have claimed the power to address an injustice.

- Reflect upon anger, evaluate your reactions and responses. Share them with a partner.

- Choose an injustice to begin to address this week.

MORE: ANGER INFORMATION

Anger is a God-given emotion. Anger is not good or bad. Anthony Robbins says anger is a signal that you need to do something. We fear anger when it's been expressed violently.

When you become angry:

- Acknowledge it. Say, "I am angry."

- Explore how it makes you feel. What do you want to do with it? The key is to *respond* to the anger, make a logical decision; not *react* without thought for the end results.

- Take the time you need to process it. Why are you angry? What happened? Is it logical to be angry about this or is it a signal that you need to work on something?

- Anger is healthy and can be used to propel us to work for justice.

- If you are angry for weeks on end it's a signal that you may need professional help.

Endurance: Moving through one day at a time is a great accomplishment in times of trial. Congratulate yourself for continuing on. Give thanks to God for ongoing support, even when you can't see it.

Assurance: Anger can be used for good (Mark 3:1–5). Honest communication can reduce anger (Ephesians 4:25). Resource: http://www.gotquestions.org/anger.html

15

The Unstoppable Setting Sun

THE MORALE OF THE choir had hit an all-time low. Our beloved music director of thirty-five years was having a difficult time at the age of eighty. I desperately wanted her to be able to fulfill her dream of directing until she died.

The music committee and I met with the personnel committee. Longtime choir members spoke earnestly of the changes needed and the pain it would cause. It was decided this needed to be an annual review with the music, choir, and personnel committees each represented but that the pastor's presence wouldn't be helpful. Three people met with Beverly.

Here she was, our spirited, determined, gifted, and aging Beverly. I knew from previous experience that when she heard the review of how things were going in the choir she would resign. Sure enough, the next day she turned in her resignation. No one was happy.

The next morning, I woke up doubled over by cramps. It hadn't been this bad since 1989! I decided to write out what was stressing me in my journal:

> Why am I stressed?
>
> A-Ted leaves early Wed a.m. for Mozambique.
>
> B-I'm going to WI. Why am I doing this? It stresses me out.
>
> C-Need a rental car for WI, hate making reservations and stuff.
>
> D-Beverly resigned. Which is awful and good at the same time.
>
> E-Our spectacular pianist and organist is leaving us for a pipe organ!
>
> F-No new prospects for organists although we've been advertising for a while.
>
> G-I keep telling everyone God will take care of it. But have trouble resting in God myself.

H-Need exercise, wanted to go bike riding but it rained and I was in pain.

I-Feel distant from my women's support group. Went for a while and then to the hospital to be with my clergysister while her husband was having surgery.

J-Dreading figuring out DMIN project paper for Church Administration Class.

K-Summer camp and there is no more childcare in place.

L- At the age of seven, my daughter has acquired an attitude worthy of puberty!

M-My treasurer is resigning at the end of the year. Huge volunteer job. Who will do it?

N-Need to plan staff training for the fall and have no new ideas.

O-Need to talk to advisor about changing dissertation project subject.

Was this enough stuff? I tried to hand all this stuff over to God, but keep taking it back from God. Oh, I missed my afternoon dose of medication.

I called my best friend, Hillary, "Hey, woman!" I said with an enthusiasm I didn't feel.

"Hi, Teresa. What's new with you today?" she asked.

"It's weird. I'm so whipped. I've been taking naps every day. Plus, I have a strange rash on my arms. I'm keeping a food journal like the dermatologist said, but it doesn't seem to be showing a pattern."

"The rash is a real mystery. The naps, isn't low energy a sign of depression?" she asked. I changed the subject by asking about her church and what was new. Then she asked about mine.

"You won't believe it. I have new people who have taken on new responsibilities. They even ran a whole event without me having to do anything," I exclaimed.

"Great. It's great you have momentum, instead of continually having to push and pull things along, like before," she applauded me.

"Want to hear my girl's latest antics?" I asked.

"Sure do," she said with a smile in her voice.

"Yesterday she was all dressed up in an old ball gown and high heels and then she picked up two sticks in the yard. She came in the house pretending to play viola with them, laughing and laughing."

We both cracked up.

❧❧❧

The August due date of my Church Administration class paper drew near, and I was panicked. We'd been tasked to try out a leadership style we had studied and then write up the results. Nothing jelled. No style was right. With leaden spirit and fingers I typed out the paper without leaving enough time for Hillary to edit it for me.

No sooner had I turned in the paper than I got word that Howard, with the heart of gold, had died. Howard reminded me every year when I needed to get my state car inspection sticker renewed. As I prepared for his funeral I asked myself, *Why do I get so attached to people? Death is too hard. Why do these people become family to me?*

After the funeral, the graveside service and the meal with the family, I changed into shorts. I headed back to the church to help rearrange choir chairs for Sunday, grabbed a bite to eat, and went to see Karla.

I reported to Karla, "Dr. Oh is concerned that I am so tired all the time, especially since low energy is a sign of depression. But we left my medication alone for now."

We turned to the matter of how deeply grieved I felt.

❧❧❧

Ted came home from Mozambique. Together we began to plan what to take on vacation. Then I went off to lead my half-day staff retreat. We'd hoped to head to the beach at two that afternoon. I came home from the retreat. Ted had eaten all the Cheetos I had packed for vacation. No one was home. There was no note telling me where they had gone.

Mentally I went *off*. I finished off my newsletter article. No word from Ted. I lay down for a nap. Around five o'clock I woke up and began to pack the rest of our stuff, grumbling all the while. The moment Ted walked in the door, I jumped on him.

"Where have you guys been?!" I demanded. Before the words were out of my mouth my daughter walked in. I could see where they had been—getting her hair relaxed.

"I took her to get her hair done," Ted answered. "The shop said they would do it in an hour. We went back in an hour. Oh no, they couldn't do it then. We went to another shop. They started to work on it but it was so tangled Helen cried and cried. It was awful," Ted told me all about it.

We pulled up to the state park gates after dark. Upon entering the park my anxiety and irritability disappeared. We swam, went to the airplane museum nearby, and ate doughnuts in the rain. We laughed, slept, and made love. Sweet.

Returning home, as soon as we pulled in the driveway, the anxiety ran out the door and grabbed me. Karla was waiting for me when I arrived at her office in a knot.

"Let's review the year," she suggested. "Teresa, this year Ted has been gone five weeks and you find single parenting stressful; you are enrolled in a doctor of ministry program and have taken four classes this year; you have been processing your sexual abuse and sharing it with people; your music director and organist have resigned; your daughter is starting public school for the first time; during the summer you were without a schedule; went to Alaska with relatives, and went to Wisconsin for seven days, which was two days too long; you also went head-to-head with your dad over 'no' meaning 'no.'"

"Okay, okay, so it has been stressful but ... " I argued.

"But nothing. Go have your annual physical and ask the doctor to check you for causes of exhaustion such as anemia and thyroid. Then go and meet with your psychiatrist with the results from your physical and discuss whether changing medication is warranted."

I went home and we had a family meeting. I was going to stop over functioning and doing all of the housework, cooking, and shopping. Ted would do the cooking on Mondays and Thursdays. My girl insisted on cooking dinner on Tuesdays.

I had planned on going on retreat the next week. Karla and I talked about how I didn't do anything at half speed. Everything was intense. Dad was like that, too.

ตะ ตะ ตะ

Every year I sweated over Christmas Eve services. This year we would have three services. How would I make it come alive this time? Then I knew what I'd do. I'd tell the story and give voice to each of the characters as if we could hear them think before they speak. I was excited. I placed the lectern just so, I practiced reading the story and stepping away from the lectern to do the pretend/acting parts.

Christmas Eve arrived. The candlelight combined with precious music created an exquisite feeling. If there was a time when I felt most alive it was not when opening the gifts on Christmas morn or Christmas dinners; it was here in the church on Christmas Eve.

The pianist played with tenderness and brightness, as if she could illustrate the birth with her fingers on the keys. The newly retired choir director had been invited to direct, and with her in directing the choir shone, mirroring the gift of Christmas. I stepped out and began to preach the Word. As I pretended to be the innkeeper, I saw the children were hooked. When I acted the part of the shepherd, I saw people crane their heads to see me and hear the words. There was a hush in the whole church.

With each successive service, the choir director and the pianist upped the ante. A dad played his guitar while his small son sang "Silent Night." The musician played "Manheim Steamroller" on the piano. Again and again the people passed the light of the world, in the form of small candles. Over and over the shimmering light filled the soft darkness and illuminated the faces of the people I'd come to love over the past seven years.

The following morning I watched our daughter tear open gifts and smile so big it was as if she were a puppet with a mouth as wide as her whole face! Later, I traipsed through the woods and inhaled the cold peace of a winter morning. The day slid by.

We left for our annual vacation between Christmas and New Year's. The mountain air brought a winter freshness; I rejoiced in the intimacy of the car ride. The goodness of our little family surrounded me, but I couldn't get in it because I felt sick. Was it the altitude? It was like morning sickness but I knew I wasn't pregnant. Slightly dizzy, nauseous, what was it? It was as if my body sensed what the year would bring.

I hauled in stacks of books to our hotel room. As the days went by, I devoured one after another. Ted and our girl reveled in cable television, indoor pools, and sledding. But I lived in the books, each story more powerful than the last. The Holy Spirit was knitting each character and bringing the dry bones to life so that I could see how it all fit and where God was at work. I was filled with God's living water, brimming, spilling over with these good gifts.

Saturday driving home, I began to struggle. Which book's story would best illustrate the text for the next sermon? I couldn't use them all—it would take too long and be too much. All night long I tossed and turned, unable to find peace and answers. It was strange because usually when I got in bed at night, the sermon melded.

As we walked up to the church, I carried the pile of books and my lack of decision. Still I prayed. No answer. Seven stories were six too many. Whatever would I do?

In the quiet before everyone arrived, I checked the answering machine, looked over the bulletin, and sat in prayer. The choir ambled in, stopped by my office with Sunday morning cheer.

"You're back!" they exclaimed with pleasure.

"How was the trip?" they asked with genuine interest.

The service began. The prayers and liturgy rolled along smoothly. The sermon time approached. I stepped up with trepidation.

This passion rose within me. I was engulfed by the Holy Spirit and I let it have its way. Enthusiasm filled me. Scripture bubbled up. The Word took over. And the seven illustrations? I preached about passion and the ability to go the distance and the illustrations of the books flowed one into the other. It was an unending sermon of joy and a deep desire to light the fires of my congregation with faith and desire to serve the Lord.

As the service ended, I saw the clock. Horror filled my heart. A forty-minute sermon. Ugh. The service had run more than an hour and a half. Gulp. That was only acceptable on special occasions. People greeted me warmly, but there was a pit in my stomach.

Each time the office phone rang that week I profusely apologized for the sermon length. Each time the person was oblivious to the sermon length and went on about the meaning of the sermon and the passion of its delivery.

My neighbor and I visited across the street while doing lawn work.

He commented, "Wow. I wish I had that kind of passion."

The board chair called and in the midst of church business, she commented, "I was just telling some folks at work about the terrific sermon."

I was baffled. But there was no time to contemplate; I was gearing up to take my January DMIN class, Monday through Friday. I was trying to do bulletin copy in advance. Hymn choices, Sunday scriptures, and checking on the hospitalized filled the time.

The following week came quickly. I was walking to my car on the way to make a visit when Aiden pulled up in his truck. We stood underneath the tall pine trees.

He spoke with difficulty and earnestness, "Some people are unhappy."

I looked him in the eye and waited, "Oh?"

"They are unhappy with your preaching. Some say if they want to see acting they will go to the theater downtown."

"Would you tell me their names so that I can visit them and we can talk about it?" I asked.

"They wanted to remain anonymous. They say if things don't change they will leave the church and take their money with them. They say they dislike everything about worship."

I stood uncertainly. "If I can't talk to them, how can I understand? If they don't come to me personally how can I take it seriously? I don't do anonymous complaints. I guess I would take it seriously if you say these are your concerns as well."

He stood still. It was as if everything were in slow motion.

"They are," he finally declared. I thanked him and assured him I would think about it. As I drove away, I was sure there were knives sticking out of my back. My friends had stabbed me.

Less than two months before, the personnel committee had reviewed my work. Not one criticism was made.

Afterwards, I'd overheard someone say, "The hymns have been kind of strange this year."

I was deeply troubled. My clergy support group breakfast was a day away.

Sliding into the booth with the guys, I offered up my anonymous complaints.

Bob, my long-term pastor friend, said, "Ahhhh. You are officially a long-term preacher!" I looked at him like he was crazy. "When you get to the seventh year, people decide either you must be exactly what they want, there is no hope you are leaving voluntarily after this long, or they must leave."

Understanding flooded my soul. Before I had come, worship had been filled with traditional music, quiet litanies, and a plain twenty-minute sermon.

Seven years prior they were living in fear that the church was dying. Now seven years later, there was life and vibrancy—I was not needed; my "style" need not be embraced or tolerated. Furthermore, the old choir director was gone and she represented balance and stability.

The new choir director was also our organist. That had made it necessary for us to relocate the choir. I was the leader, therefore it was my fault.

It didn't matter that no one had applied to be organist. It only mattered that I was the figurehead and these changes happened during my tenure.

During my DMIN class, I mulled over the dynamics of the last seven years and the alienation some people had to be feeling. I resolved I wouldn't do any more dramatic sermons unless someone asked for one. No one did. I resolved to "settle down some" and it began to kill me. The stab wounds ached and bled in the night.

Bo was making bulletin errors and people were complaining. I failed to see the cyclical nature of it all and tried to corral her hours so that adequate bulletin proofing could occur.

She argued with me, "It's been working this way—what's the problem?" Bo continued to finish things at midnight on Saturday. The office lost its camaraderie. Morale fell. I tried repeatedly to talk to Bo. I grew red and stumbled. She argued. I gave up and wrote a written warning. She was indignant. The weeks straggled along. I fell into a place of deep anxiety.

I took the phone call from a police officer in the middle of a meeting. Dee, one of my dearest church supporters, had had a heart attack!

I rushed to get to the hospital. Part way there I realized I had no cash and it was a toll road. I took an alternate route but it was dark and I was upset. Then I was lost and upset. By the time I arrived, she had died. Her daughter and I, the whole family, gathered and wept and planned and prayed. On the way home, I mourned the loss of one of my biggest cheerleaders.

That night I called my mother just to hear her voice and feel comforted.

"Hey, Mom! What's new with you?" I asked her, trying to distract myself.

She sighed, "It's not good. Your aunt was four-wheeling with her mother and they turned onto the highway to go to the trail. A semi-truck came up over the hill. Her mother's four-wheeler ran straight into the semi." Our conversation trailed off. I hung up comfortless.

I told Ted about it. I didn't know if I had the story right. I did know I had a funeral to conduct and a burial to oversee.

During the service we poured out our love for Dee with lavishness. I drove alone to the cemetery, an hour and a half away. Every semi that passed by made me wonder what it was like to be run over by one. At the graveside, people said they had passed me on the highway and waved, but

I didn't even see them. I couldn't tell them about my separate trauma; it wasn't appropriate.

I tried to hike on the mountain path nearby but ran into bears. I took another trail and pushed myself hard. It didn't matter. I couldn't lose the grief. I went to a friend's house for a quick lunch. She was solicitous as always.

"What would you like?" I took some water and declined food. I was not able to say what I wanted. On the drive home, a blue funk filled me.

Weeks passed by. Bo didn't stay on task with deadlines. I had written her up a second time. I had gone to Elmer repeatedly seeking advice.

Winter bled into spring. Woodenly, I went through the motions of preaching. No one spoke of anonymous complainers anymore. I was anxious over stupid things. Karla suggested I talk with Dr. Oh about some kind of anxiety med to use only as needed.

Dr. Oh said, "Meds aren't meant to protect you from the ups and downs of life" or something like that.

Taking the stairs out of the building, I muttered, "You didn't hear me. You don't hear me. You don't want to hear me. I hate you."

The green of summer had burst into being everywhere but in my stony heart. I had sealed it up like a tomb. But hope shone on the horizon in the form of a trip to Switzerland.

Ted asked me over and over again, "Where do you want to go while we are there? What do you want to do? Have you called your family members and contacted your distant relatives?" Forever I had longed to see Switzerland, to be there. But I was unable to give answers. Irritated that he kept asking, I got short with him.

"I don't know. Plan what you plan." Call relatives? I hated cold calls. Ask an aunt where she went and how she knew where to go? Too hard. My anxiety rose higher.

Planning meetings took place for the women's conference group I facilitated. The women talked over top of each other. It grated on me. I volunteered to do a workshop. This would be the third or fourth year I'd done one on suffering. Almost every time, the workshops were filled to capacity.

Not wanting to fall behind in my DMIN studies, I undertook a summer independent study on the Psalms with one of the brightest exegetical professors. I had found my life story in this five thousand year old poetry, the lament Psalms. Now I was going to examine some of them with intentionality. But it had been twenty years since I'd done scholarly exegesis and I was scared stiff.

I sat in the seminary library and brooded. I was sick of feeling clingy and worrying about the return of the monster, depression. I was tired: of being envious of Ted's new appointment, of the treadmill of life, of constantly researching suffering.

Instead of doing research, I wrote out my thoughts:

Why should I care if other people suffer? I suffered and lived through it. Why do I want to subject myself to stretching and learning? I want to curl in a ball and hold myself tight crying long into the night.

I got free of the childhood suffering and bounced through the school years—undergraduate, graduate, and into life only to free-fall into depression. I decided after the second, or was it the third? clinical depression (freefall) to wear a harness, to attach myself to a safety net—antidepressants for the rest of my life. For a time my decision had carried me well. It held me in check long enough to develop friendships and lifelines and live through Karla's departure from the area.

I long to not be bored, but rather be stretched by the DMIN program. I want to be about the business of saving others, not just myself. I want to know what new counselor I can see that will be perfect, without all the work. I want to be clear about how I am and whose I am.

This ministry, family, degree, project, and paper has claimed me and named me, shaped me and shifted me. This was an immersion, not a choice. This was my life, not a thing I got to pick. This was my brain with not enough chemicals. This was my family history—not knowing how to make friends, not knowing I had worth. This suffering came to me; I did not seek it out.

I come to myself and find my life has been a journey of purpose, worth, healing, and hope. I know this is life. This is my life. I have come to embrace myself and my past. I have come to map out the way to peace and peacefulness for myself and others.

Nailing my tail down to the chair I began to write out the exegesis paper:

The following exegesis of three lament psalms (88, 59, and 77) traces the prevalence of human suffering back through time connecting us to God and one another. The process of exegesis serves to find theological themes and reflect on prayers of suffering in detail. My prayer is for this body of exegetical work to be transformed into Holy instruction from God as my brothers and sisters preach The Word.

"Laments (when we feel God is absent) can serve to draw us nearer and experience God's presence. When this happens, the lament usually ends in praise such as in Psalms 59 and 77. However, there are Psalms of lament, such as Psalm 88, in which the writer cries out against the injustice and the agony of suffering without ending in praise. Truly, the laments are a demonstration of God's love and commitment to human freedom, especially the freedom of speech."

I'd found myself in Psalm 88. The sufferer had nothing to lose. He or she was in utter, agonizing, unrelenting pain. The suffering had been lifelong or so it seemed. Dr. Aaron Beck, the physician who first diagnosed clinical depression, could have used Psalm 88 as a classic example of what's called Beck's Triad Syndrome. Beck's Triad Syndrome is a condition of the brain where the person cannot remember a time when life was good, nor can they envision life will ever be any different than the present.

Psalm 59 made me believe that five thousand years ago people had suffered from repetitive spinning thoughts like I had. Psalm 77 helped me to understand that a tight focus on suffering excludes all else. It showed me that when one considered the big picture, one could see God at work. I was amazed that no one had ever shared the lament Psalms with me.

Finishing up the paper on three psalms of lament was an incredibly freeing feeling. I could go off to Switzerland without coming back to the paper.

Switzerland came. Cold glacier water sluiced through the mountains. We rode the zip wire down the side of a mountain because it was too slushy to ride dogsleds. I was Heidi on the Alps. I was Alice in Wonderland. I was removed from anxiety through a time machine.

SLAYING THE MONSTER

- What sorts of things did Teresa lose perspective on as she became more depressed?

- When you are anxious, what makes a difference for you?

- Have you ever been depressed? Do you know people who are depressed? Share what it is like. Share the hope you have found.

MORE: ANXIETY AND STRESS INFORMATION

The Signs of Depression are listed in the front of the book.

One in Four people experience depression. Counseling and medication are effective but require time and effort, as well as adjustments from time to time. For an easy-to-read, helpful book about depression, check out *Undoing Depression* by Dr. Richard O'Connor.

Anxiety and Stress can be helped. Check out Richard O'Connor's book, *Undoing Perpetual Stress: The Missing Connection between Depression, Anxiety and the 21st Century Illness.*

Anxiety is excitement and passion misdirected.

Stress is the result of taking on too much, having unrealistic expectations of oneself, or being with someone who has unrealistic expectations of you. Being perfect, doing all things right or well is unrealistic. We are made by God to be human. If humans were perfect they would be God.

Assurance: Cast your cares upon God (1 Peter 5:7). Anxiety weighs you down (Proverbs 12:25). Let go of anxiety (I Corinthians 7:32). Trust God to provide (Luke 12:27).

16

Stumbling in the Dark

MY COUNSELOR, KARLA HAD moved. I was loathe to try and find another counselor so did nothing for months, except take daily naps. A bad sign. Finally, I forced myself to go and see a new counselor, Carol.

Small things seemed too large to tackle. I was weary, very weary. September arrived. Ted and I were walking to the local diner for dinner.

As we crossed the yard, I opened the packet containing my church administration paper.

"Oh no! She gave me a B-," I cried out.

Ted put his arm around me and said, "You passed. It's a passing grade. That's all that matters."

"Look at the remarks she wrote," I moaned.

"Your writing needs great improvement. You failed to do the assignment as assigned. Your grammar is atrocious."

I carried my weary butt in to see Dr. Oh—she upped the dosage a little on my meds. A month went by.

I pushed myself through the door of Carol's office and came clean between bursts of tears. "Every Sunday when I stand up to preach, my brain says, 'I can't do this.'"

For the nearly twenty years I'd been in counseling off and on, I'd never told anyone the thoughts that ran through my mind. "I can't tell you how often my brain says to me, 'You might as well be dead,'" I reported to Carol. "I want to stop these unrelenting messages. I want out. I want to lop off my head and run away from it. I can't live like this." I told her of all the commitments I had coming up. "I can't do this anymore." When the tears gave out, Carol leaned forward and looked me in the eye.

"You need to take some time off. This is like having a severe case of the flu. Take the week off. Do not do the workshop this weekend. Do not volunteer at the conference. Do not preach on Sunday. Stay in bed. Drink fluids. Rest. Treat it like the flu—a bad case of the flu."

I walked out snuffling, shuffling in the bright sunshine. I'd always feared I would fall apart. This was it. How could I tell the ladies at the conference that I couldn't do it? I was supposed to go there and unpack the mission table.

I carried the heavy bag with all the conference materials into the host site. Pat and Roberta were nearest to the door. I rested the bag on a chair and fought for words, some words, any words. No words, only tears. Damn the tears!

"I'm clinically depressed," I finally stammered. "I've been told I need rest. I can't be here today or tomorrow." I closed my eyes tightly, trying to stop the flow of tears, trying to gather the words that were scattered everywhere. "I need to resign as facilitator. Here are all of the materials."

They murmured motherly things to me, assuring me I would be all right. "Take care of yourself," they said.

At home, I crawled under my blankets and cried myself to sleep. When I awoke, the sun was covering my bed. I was alone in my head. My head spun the same thoughts around and around like a dryer that never stopped. *What was the point of living? I couldn't do anything right. I might as well be dead. I was helpless.*

I slept again. Upon awaking the thoughts assaulted me. *How could this be? I'd taken my medicine and seen the psychiatrist every three months, more often when feeling rotten. I had been to counseling every other week, now every week. How could this have happened again?* Underneath the exhaustion, a small voice said, "*It's your fault! You knew things were off.*"

I argued with the small voice. *I told my counselor and she told me to ask the psychiatrist for something to take the edge off of my anxiety. My psychiatrist upped something but didn't give me anything for anxiety.*

The Welbutrin had been working perfectly. I hadn't gained weight. I had achieved a normal level of energy. When did it stop working for me? Why did it stop working? What was wrong with me?

Everything was in slow motion and detached. Ted found me in bed. I told him about this "flu." Focus-man Smith flew into action. He took notes, wrote down details. My daughter came and hugged me. I felt sadness. My husband checked on me. I felt failure.

I had to decide what to tell the congregation. Ted walked me through the decision making process, volunteered to preach for me.

"Just tell them I'm sick and need rest."

He called Aiden and Elmer.

Tears connected the freckles on my face and rolled into my ears. My pillow was soggy. I cried out to God, *Why me? Why did I have to go through all this? Haven't I been through enough? Where are you, God? Why do you allow this? What were you thinking? How can we say you are a loving God and a gentle shepherd? Who started telling me that lie? Why?*

Negative thoughts streamed through my brain, *You've been much worse off and you didn't take time off then. Why take time off this time? You don't deserve this.*

A half hour before bed my girl and I read stories and cuddled. Hillary came over to play Scrabble, but I didn't enjoy it.

I talked to my friend Juanita for fifteen minutes and set up lunch with her and dinner with Cat on Wednesday. Within an hour I knew I'd have to cancel one or the other. Going out for one meal would wear me out.

On Monday I had lunch with another friend, Maggie. As usual she was dressed to the nines—lovely scarf, perfect hair and makeup. She zipped in chattering a mile a minute. That was Maggie.

Partway into lunch she asked me, "What's it like to be depressed?"

I told her, "My brain keeps saying, 'I can't do this.' I might as well be dead.'"

The more I told her, the deeper Maggie seemed to sink. It was like she had tied her thoughts so closely to mine in trying to understand that she was being pulled into the pit with me. I left lunch feeling worse.

The next day, I was to lead mentoring activities at a retreat center a few hours away. I called Aria, one of the event planners.

"Aria, I took Sunday off because I was so depressed."

She asked me, "How did you do that?"

"I don't think I can make it to the retreat."

When I hung up the phone, I knew Aria didn't understand I was saying I was too sick to come. Ted and I talked.

"I don't want to have to talk to the coordinator about it," I moaned. "I already feel bad; I don't need anyone to make me feel worse."

"Send him an email," Ted suggested. "He's vigilant about checking emails. He checks them late at night and early in the morning."

I sent the email. "I am sick and not able to come. I apologize for the inconvenience." When I pushed send I felt both free and sick at the same time. I was free of the overwhelming idea of facing sixty people and leading them. I was sick to have forgone a responsibility, one I had been excited about taking on.

Tuesday came. I took my morning nap. After lunch, I straightened up the work shed and took my afternoon nap. The day passed.

Around dinnertime the phone rang, a frantic voice was on the phone. "Teresa!"

"Yes?"

"Are you on your way? We need you here!" It was the coordinator. My mouth was dry.

"I sent an email. I'm too sick to come," I said.

"Email?" the coordinator exclaimed. "I've been at the retreat center since last night; I haven't had a chance to see my email. I don't know what we'll do. We need you here."

I apologized.

"Well, I've got to go and figure out what we are going to do. I wish you had called me. Goodbye," he said and hung up.

The feeling of illness lingered all evening. I beat myself up. I was responsible and had blown it.

Wednesday came. I did laundry and cooked, all the while crying. What was I going to do? I was in knots. I couldn't stop worrying about next week and re-entering the workplace. My house felt like a psychiatric ward; I shuffled around in slippers, dull eyed.

Finally I wrote a letter to the key leaders and told them of my clinical depression and let them know I wouldn't be there on Sunday. They left me a phone message. "We'll take care of church on Sunday. Get your rest so you can get well."

The message made me cry. I felt helpless and sick. Sick and helpless. My pride hurt.

I wrote out forty cards for a friend's fortieth birthday. Thursday I planted flower bulbs and cancelled lunch with Juanita. At one o'clock I saw Carol. I sank into the couch. Words I did not have, only tears. She waited for my tears to stop. My words leaked out like tears.

"I'm . . . I took time off. Why don't I feel better? What's wrong with me?"

She assured me, "You've taken time off. You're taking care of yourself—that's good. It's important. One step at a time. You'll know when it's time to go back to work, when you can't stand being at home, when your energy level increases."

"When? How long is it going to take?"

I left in a fog. I needed to communicate with my leaders. I shut down at this overwhelming thought. Lying down on the couch, I slept the sleep of the disturbed.

Waking up in time to get my daughter from school, I walked through the neighborhood. I hoped no one would see me. What would I say? I didn't look sick from the outside. How did you explain depression?

I went through the side gate at school and tried to pick her up without speaking to anyone. I slid between people and under conversations. As we walked home, I tried to talk with her like normal. "How was your day?"

She told me about her two friends, "Joannie and Julie both wanted to play with me, by themselves." I was jealous and unequipped. I'd never been popular. Even if my brain were working right, I wouldn't know what to say.

Relieved to get home, I lay down while she got herself a snack. The days passed one by one. I slept. I ate. I picked up our daughter from school. I beat myself up.

It had been ten days. I told Carol about my naps and irritability.

"That means you aren't ready to go back, take another week off," said Carol.

Cat drove two hours just to have dinner with me. We laughed really hard. I told her the whole story. She encouraged me not to rush back to work.

"It took a long time to go down into the pit so it will take time to get back up. It takes time to give birth to a new self," Cat shared with me.

I said a little prayer, *Thank you, God, for Cat.*

Monday I tried to nap. Couldn't. Read a book. I took my turn with aftercare at school. We puddle splashed on the way home and ate butternut squash for supper. Ted came home late and we made love. Best in a long time.

Tuesday I found myself humming and smiling! Wow.

At aftercare, I worked with a child. I felt positively cheerful, bouncy, and conversational. I was thinking about going back to work. "I think I can . . . . I think I can . . ." like *The Little Engine that Could.* I tried to call Elmer, the Personnel chair. His wife called me back—he was in the hospital needing bypass surgery! I checked my email and found out they were interviewing potential secretaries. Bo had quit a month or so before I got sick. I emailed back, said I would be there. I would check references.

Ted would visit Elmer in the hospital tomorrow. I zoned out playing Scrabble on the computer and finally went to bed. Then I got scared. I was scared of doing interviews. I was upset about checking references. I was tense and crying; Ted came and held me close. I couldn't sleep.

I was upset that I was upset and crying for the first time in nearly a week! I kept telling myself that the annual business meeting was over; church life was slower. I'd be okay.

One day Carol asked me specifically about my medication. I reviewed the history of it.

"What? Oh no. The medication from that time frame should have taken effect. You need to go see Dr. Oh immediately," Carol said.

I made the appointment.

Seeing Dr. Oh was agonizing.

"I . . . I've been on leave from work. My counselor said I should take time off . . ." I confessed.

"What?" Dr Oh interrupted me. "You've been so depressed you're not working but you didn't come and see me?" Her words were like being kicked.

Immediately I was given new prescriptions and increases in meds. I hated medications. I did not want new meds or more meds. I wanted to be healed. I wanted to be understood.

As I took the stairs out of the building I vowed that when I was a little better I would end this craziness with her and find a new psychiatrist. Carol and I began the conversation immediately. What did I want in a doctor? I wanted one that empathized. I wanted one that responded and was quick with medication changes as they were warranted.

The phone had rung repeatedly. People were leaving cheery messages.

"You've got to tell the church something," Ted told me. I sat at the computer and dully contemplated my choices. I thought one Sunday off would do it. It didn't do it. If possible I had less energy than before. I was not a rolling stone. Rock, immovable rock, was what I had become.

Writing words had always come easy to me. But now, even that skill betrayed me. "Dear leaders . . ." I tried to write, then I gave up and began to journal instead:

Sad tired discouraged teary sad achy sad want to leave want to stay scared scared of finances scared of moving uneasy about parsonage and leaving it and the shape it is in. Sad about our dog not listening and eating off my table. Sad about the gray day. No energy. Tired. Very tired. Did I say I have no energy?

I really want to feel rested. Instead I am a broken shovel. Not broken slowly, simply snapped. Unable to put myself back together. Unable to do what used to be easy to do. Broken. No leverage. No handle on anything. Sharp yet dull. Strong but weak. Tired but tough. Broken but not thrown away. Achy but not dead. What is this human stuff? Why am I made this way? What do other people do with their sadness and grief? What should I do with it? Who am I?

Aiden stopped by the house one day. He had a book to loan me.

"My daughter left her women's study class books for me to read," he said. "I thought you might find this one helpful." He left a copy of Christiane Northrup's book, *Women's Bodies, Women's Wisdom* with me.

In November of 2003 I wrote a letter to the congregation and sent a copy of it to my superintendent explaining that I had a history of depression and that I was home while I got my medications balanced. With great defeat, I emailed the letter. Then I emailed a note to the Personnel Committee Interview Team chair that I wouldn't be at the interview but I'd trust their judgment. But if the person selected was not a good match, I reserved the right to terminate him or her.

From the return emails, it seemed we were in agreement. I did not see the fight to come.

Now that my depression was public knowledge, I collapsed in a different way. The emotional toll of being transparent was huge. Would the congregation decide I was too broken to return to good health, make decisions, and lead them?

I made a decision. I would go back the last Sunday of November. I would begin reentry in December, working part time then gradually becoming full time by January.

I was sleeping less. Reading Northrup's book was helpful. She had exercises and reflections built into it that made me think hard about what I thought and believed. Meals were dropped off and I relished the warm food and good nutrition—love made tangible and edible. Cards of love and kindness piled up around me. Lassie, my dog, and I took long walks.

December and my return to work arrived. The new secretary's name was Monica. She was Souuuthern in accent and approach. Not one single direct thing about her. I was in my office part time these days.

She called out to me, "Teresa?"

I stood in front of her desk.

"I can't find the files you asked for. What would they be listed under in the computer?"

She was so good at what she did (asking for help), that I pulled up a chair and gazed at the screen as if I knew the previous secretary's filing system or even how to search for files! When I scooted back the chair I was baffled. I thought she'd had computer experience.

"You'll have to call Bo," I said finally.

One o'clock rolled around and she headed out for the day. I sighed. At least now I could get some of my own work done. Bee, the church caretaker, came down the hall using the dust mop.

"Hey!" I called out to her.

She stopped in my doorway, "Why, Teresa, it's good to see you."

"Likewise. I haven't seen you around much," I said.

"No, I make it a habit not to be here when Monica is here. I can't stand that woman!"

"Why? What's going on?" I asked.

She shook her head slowly. "Every time I get home from running errands there's a message telling me to call her! I can't help her with her computer problems." I heard her out and mulled over the issues.

The next day I strolled through the preschool, greeting the children and waving to the teachers. The halls were filled with artwork of Jesus. I stopped by the director's office and pulled up a chair to shoot the breeze.

"I don't see you upstairs much anymore," I said.

She turned, smiled and said, "Noooooooooo way." Noticing the baffled look on my face, she explained, "You know I used to be a secretary; well I have tried to help that woman repeatedly. She just doesn't get it. She doesn't learn. She gets confused about the simplest things. I make it a point to get all my copying done before she comes in to work so I don't get sucked into something."

It was a new year and a new roster was needed for the community ministers' daycare devotions. On Monday I gave Monica the old one, marked up with changes and asked her to make up a new one. It needed to be sent out within two days. Three previous secretaries I'd worked with had been able to accomplish the task in less than two hours. On Wednesday, I asked her how it was coming along.

"Oh, here it is. I'm unhappy with the big spaces at the end but I can't figure out how to reduce them," she explained.

"We don't have time to work on it anymore. This is important information, please send it out 'as is' today," I said firmly.

On Thursday morning I asked her for the bulletin to proofread it. The protocol was that a rough draft was to be done before the end of business on Wednesday.

"It's not ready yet, I'm still working on the roster for you," she said innocently.

"The roster needed to be sent out yesterday," I replied. "Please send it out today. The bulletin copy needs to be done today as well," I insisted and then retreated to my office.

Stopping by the office hours later, I said, "I'm off to the hospital to make a visit. When I come back I'll need the bulletin."

She managed to get it done. The weekend was uneventful.

"Good morning, Monica!" I called out Monday morning. "How was your weekend?"

"Oh my goodness, you won't believe it," she began. Then she proceeded to tell me about her kids, dogs, husband, and arthritis. Sitting in her office, I noticed a stack of papers on the work table. I picked one up. It was the roster that needed to be sent out last week!

"Why didn't you send out the roster?" I asked with a pained look.

"Oh ... I ... Well, I couldn't get the computer to make the spaces even and I didn't want it sent out like that." She squirmed a little bit but mostly seemed comfortable with her failure to follow repeated instructions.

"Mail it out, 'as is' immediately, today," I ordered.

Close to quitting time, I entered her office. The roster was untouched.

"Monica, I believe that you are trying but it isn't working. Please turn in your resignation effective immediately."

She turned to me with a bright smile and laid down her trump card, "I believe I'll take it up with the Personnel Committee."

I called a Personnel Committee meeting. As I explained the situation I could see the women were in agreement with me. However, one man declared it "unchristian" to fire her and then questioned my judgment given my recent recovery. The men sided with him. After seven years through thick and thin, the men did not trust my judgment. I let the decision go and handed the supervision of Monica completely over to the committee.

At home I wrestled, prayed, and talked it over with Ted. It was time for me to go to another church.

SLAYING THE MONSTER

- Consider the acronym SLAY—See, Learn, Act, Yes. Trace the four steps through one of the characters in this chapter.
- What new awareness did a person gain or see?
- What did he or she do to address what had been seen? What learning took place?
- After research, what action was taken?
- Did you see confirmation that it was the right action? Did anybody affirm themselves for making a positive change?

MORE: MEDICATION INFORMATION

Medication Information: There are a number of effective anti-depressants with low side effects. When beginning an anti-depressant, the physician will likely put the person on a half dose then step up to a full dose of medication. Side effects are the most prominent in the first few weeks. The body then grows accustomed to the medication, and the majority of side effects subside.

Within a couple of weeks, the patient will begin to feel the effects of the medication. However, the full effect of the medication takes some time to achieve. Every person is different; it takes trial and error to arrive at the right medication(s) with an effective dosage.

The human body has a tendency to acclimate to medications, causing some medications to become less effective over time. Psychiatrists only write prescriptions for three months at a time. This helps catch changes in medication effectiveness early. Some psychiatrists, called pharmacologists specialize in brain medication.

Medication and Christian Belief: If I break my wrist, I go to the hospital for treatment. I may have a cast and take antibiotics. If my brain is broken and interferes with day to day living, I believe I should use every resource available to bring healing. God provides many paths to healing: medication, visualization, healing prayer, nutrition, exercise, Bible study, massage, and more. God designed us for community, not to go it alone or pull ourselves up by our own bootstraps. God designed the world such that healing occurs via many people, methods and things working together.

Assurance: God will help you rest (Isaiah 14:3). Jesus used something besides his faith and hands (clay or mud) when healing the blind man (John 9:1–6).

17

Midnight and a Million Prayers

THE FEBRUARY PERSONNEL MEETING was called to order. The ordinary joking was long gone. There'd been too much dissension.

I took a deep breath and said, "I'm asking for a move to another church."

Immediately, one of the members stood up, shook my hand and said, "Well, it's been a good run!"

Some of the members were shocked.

"Teresa, are you sure?"

"We'd like you to stay."

We planned for the transition. I began preparing to meet with my superintendent. Doug had long since retired. This would be my first move under my current superintendent. I dressed carefully; I wanted to project professionalism without intimidation. I'd practiced what I wanted to say and how to say it. I needed to project and inspire confidence but not rattle my superintendent.

"Teresa," the superintendent responded to my request for a move, "I'd consider you for a larger church but I need to know if you're willing to take a salary cut. Because you're requesting special location in order to stay in the area, instead of being willing to be assigned anywhere within the Virginia Conference you can expect to receive a lateral appointment or a salary cut."

"I don't understand," I said. I knew other colleagues with special location requests hadn't been given a lateral move or a cut. "Are you displeased with my work? Surely there is somewhere you could and would send me within the one hundred churches here in northern Virginia."

The superintendent remained firm. When I walked out the door, I didn't let it slam me. I started slamming myself, *Teresa you knew better than to expect them to have confidence in you or to treat you like a person of worth with skills and abilities. All the crafting in the world doesn't change the reality of sexism in the world.*

Ted and I talked; he said he'd put in a word for me when he met with the superintendent. But before that could happen the superintendent showed up for Sunday worship.

It was as if all the stars in heaven had lined up that day. The children sang like angels. At children's time, I told the story about the wedding and the six women with extra oil for their lamps who would get to attend the wedding.

"Who will be the groom?" I asked. A boy volunteered.

"Who will be the bride?" I asked. No one volunteered. I turned to the congregation, "Who will be the bride?" The boy's mother volunteered. I handed out paper "lamps" to everyone else. The congregation started to hum the wedding march as the bride and groom made their way down the aisle.

When the couple was half way to the front, I said to the children with the lamps, "Quick, look on the back of your lamp. Does it have extra oil? If it doesn't have a picture of a bottle of oil, you need to run to the ushers to get more oil."

The children who needed oil pushed past the bride and groom to get to the ushers. The bride and groom arrived and I pretended to shut the door. The children who had run off to get oil came to me.

"Let us in!" they said. I shook my head.

"The story in the Bible says the ones who weren't ready, didn't get to go in to the party." Together we said a prayer and the children went off to children's church. But the congregation sat in a hush, as the reality of the judgment to come sank in. The Chancel Choir anthem soared. It was as if the Holy Spirit had filled up every nook and cranny and burst open the doors.

At my next meeting with the superintendent, he'd had a change of heart. "Teresa, there are two churches that might become available to send you to. It's a waiting game right now," he said.

After the meeting I told Ted I already knew what would happen. There was one predictable appointment that required no risk and was a nice step, an increase in salary and responsibility, but not a jump. Not an insult but a reasonable thing to do. It was the church that had already been served by two minority pastors and done well. It was a church that would increase my salary by five thousand dollars, but no more. It was a church that was stable but surrounded by great growth. It was a fine church.

Sure enough, it came to pass.

∾ ∾ ∾

The new church had exquisite stained glass windows in blues and purples bringing the Bible stories to life. Outside, the memorial gardens waved with beauty. Inside there was a sound preschool and a good choir.

I was all too happy to be leaving the place that had given me heartbreak after the happy years we'd had together. But barely had I moved into the new office when the lobbying began.

"Let me tell you the story behind the desk. You won't move it out of the office will you?"

"You aren't going to change anything, are you?"

"What? You bought your own house and you're not living in our parsonage?" (The parsonage back yard was the church parking lot).

"I'm not sure it's a good idea for you to attend all the meetings; the other preacher didn't do it that way."

The Personnel Committee had their first meeting, "Teresa, we need staff unity. If you could work to increase morale, that would be great. We've scheduled a continuing education event for the entire staff. The speaker is an expert in conflict mediation. Truth be told, we've had some conflicts that weren't handled in the best way."

I brought in long-time members and asked them to tell me about the church. I went to lunch at people's homes and heard their dreams and heartbreaks about the church. They went out of the way to welcome my daughter. I was grateful and touched by the tea party they held for her to meet the other girls her age.

Carol and I talked at length about the church.

She asked, "What do you expect to happen?"

"I expect, if I do my best, and work hard, within a year everyone will be working together. It's always worked like that in the past. The only thing different is that I expect that I can and should be myself, instead of trying to please every person—bending myself back and forth to the breaking point like I've done in the past. I expect God will work through me and these people to bring about life and ministry."

I'd hardly begun before I was weary. Where was my heart for ministry? Where was the warmth and welcome of the congregation that I'd experienced elsewhere?

All around me was shifting sand. From day to day the dunes changed places and any oasis was replaced by a mirage. Morale proved elusive at best. I sought out guidance regularly. I tried their way. I tried my way. I tried other ways. At every turn I was met with resistance and resentment.

There was a herd of sacred cows, age-old traditions. I couldn't see them and the congregation couldn't name them unless I tripped over one. Then a bellow arose from the herd and before I could move or understand, a stampede was underway.

For a full year, I held my ear to the ground. I listened and tried to learn. What I learned was that factions were forming among the long-time members. What I understood was that new people were pouring in the doors. Many members were excited, willing and interested in serving.

The second year a riptide was formed by human hands of unresolved conflict, things deemed unmentionable, and much more churned along daily. One staff person resigned. A second person turned in her resignation. The new person was spun to and fro like a yoyo by the new situation.

Carol listened and listened. Week after week she listened as my stomach churned and my sense of defeat grew. Week after week she reframed situations to show me how it wasn't all personal. There were other things happening, or that had happened years ago, that were shaping people's responses.

Desperate about the way Ted and I were gaining weight, I asked Ted, "Will you pray about walking a marathon with me?" A couple of days later I asked what his answer was.

"I'll do the marathon with you, if you complete your dissertation and graduate."

∾∾∾

With joy, Ted held my hand as we crossed the finish line in less than eight hours. After training for five months, we had walked 26.2 miles. I signed up for two DMIN classes: God, Providence, and Evil; and Church Leadership.

Dr. Kendall Soulen led us through the spectrum of thought on God's providence and the presence of evil. He pointed out Marilyn McCord Adams' definition of suffering, "Suffering is when the meaning or purpose of your life is destroyed." We read McCord Adams' caveat, "The only person who can determine if you are suffering is you." The class was challenged to reflect on what they believed about God, about God and suffering, about God and evil, and more. In this way I learned holy conferencing–the ability to share where one stood presently without having to prove one was right.

I met with my advisor about my dissertation, "I need help with the wording of my question." I told him. There at the table that filled most of his office, we tried out phrase after phrase.

"Tell me again, what is it you want to do?" he said.

"I believe that Christians have bought into the common American belief that suffering is optional and irregular, un-American. America says either 'Get the problem fixed' or 'Be quiet.'

We've trained people to bottle up their suffering. We've lost our way when it comes to caring for those who grieve. We are uncomfortable with their grief, so we want them to be well. If they can't be well then they should at least act as if they were well."

"Okay, I'm with you so far." My advisor nodded.

"I propose that I find other pastors who will preach a three Sunday sermon series on suffering using three Psalms of lament that I've researched."

"Good. Good." My advisor picked up where I'd left off. "Teresa, I think you're on to something. Recruit pastors from different areas to preach the series. Teach the pastors the material. Have the congregants fill out a simple response card."

My eyes lit up, "This is doable. Can I help people learn the lessons found in the lament Psalms, help them form a theology of suffering?"

I went home and sent out an email invitation to hundreds of my fellow pastors. No one responded to the invitation to preach the series.

At the bookstore, I ran into Gary, "Hey, man! What's new?" Gary filled me in on his canoe trip and the thrill of leading the group. Then I told him my dilemma.

"I need colleagues to preach a three part sermon series with me."

"I'd be honored to do it with you." He volunteered, then suggested I call his friend Nancy, to see if she'd be willing to participate. I was psyched. Nancy served little churches up on the West Virginia state line. Gary served a county seat church.

On the drive home, it came to me. Ileana would do it. She'd help me. Sure enough she said yes, she would preach the series to her congregation made up of first generation Spanish speaking immigrants.

My official dissertation question was: "Can I create a model for preaching the Psalms of lament in a way that moves congregants from cultural forms of denial of suffering to a biblical theology of communicating suffering?"

Months passed. The series were preached and the response cards began arriving in the mail. First up was Gary's packet. At the door, after the church service a woman had approached him and told him her story.

"The sermon about praying constantly happened the same day my father was killed in an accident. The peace I received through constant prayer was so clear and amazing to me. It was stunning. For forty years, I had lived in fear of the death of a parent. My fear melted away in the comfort and calm of the Psalm and I was able to go on through that which I had lived in dread of for so long."

Comments poured in. A person wrote that he had read the lament Psalms for sanity and related to the anger and feeling of forsakenness during his daughter's teenage years. One person shared that the sermons based on the lament Psalms had helped them realize their faith was based on a true feeling of God.

One of my congregants shared, "I have come to believe that God's grace and presence is in my life through the lives of those around me who influence me continually and faith in God's active intervention in my life. The sermons have helped define and explain so many events in my life. Thank you. Keep 'em comin.'"

Others responded thoughtfully, "I have learned a new concept." "By experience, I know God is with me. God makes me know I am not alone. I am lifted up and restored." I gathered up the cards that were positive and the ones that were unusual, "I found the series depressing." "I am eighty-one years old and have never suffered."

❧ ❧ ❧

A generous woman gave me her beach front condo for a week in order to focus on finishing my paper. Cat came down and spent the night.

"Will you proofread it for me?" I asked her.

She sat on the floor and spread the paper out on the coffee table to read my first page:

"Once, in a Bible Study a man said that I was like Jacob, always wrestling. Indeed, it was true at the age of twenty-five. It is true now. I introduce you to a part of my soul. A part I had walled off so well I did not know it existed.

"I believe every person's story can be found in the Bible. Someone found me in the Jacob wrestling with an angel story, the one where he comes away with a permanent limp (Genesis 32). I found myself in the Psalms of lament. I did not want to find myself there. No one does. That is precisely the problem.

"No one looks for the valley of the shadow of death and the suffering stumbling stories that unfold there. We soothe ourselves with the twenty-third Psalm, skipping past the darkness, like a child staying on the sunny side of the street. Only when you've walked on the other side, only when you have been forced to sup with your worst fears and dangerous nightmares, can you speak with authenticity. Who wants that authority?

"I have come forward to speak for those who are eating now, at a terrible table. I have written for those for whom the phrase, 'How are you?' slices like a knife in the night. Who needs it? The ones who have not walked where some of us have walked. The ones who care for the suffering and get so caught in our painful stories, they sink like a stone with us.

"Stop. Learn the lessons of the Psalms of lament. Learn to not only listen. Learn to lift up the suffering one, not so much the suffering. In the words of Dr. Bruce Birch, Professor of Old Testament at Wesley Theological Seminary, and one who has feasted at that terrible table:

Show us the pathways into the future when we do not see them ourselves . . . [Do this] by receiving our pain and our loss, but also by refusing to believe that such pain and loss constitute the final word.

"Teresa," Cat called out. "You need to make sure to footnote the Birch quote as having come from *The Christian Century*, 'Biblical Faith and the Loss of Children,' (26 October 1983)."

When Cat left, another dear friend, Lynne arrived to bolster my confidence. I returned home with the paper mostly done and a deep sense of gratitude.

With my dissertation turned in I was better able to hear Carol's advice.

"Leave this church. For the sake of your health find a different job." I argued with her. There was no guarantee I wouldn't encounter the same conflict in another church.

A year before, in the midst of crisis I had sought out a spiritual director.

Now, I went to see her and she echoed Carol's opinion, using different words, "You are spiritually empty. You have nothing left to give. To stay at your current church is unthinkable."

I went straight home and told Ted about it. I expected he would say, "You're strong. You'll be fine."

But Ted said, "Do it. Take a year off."

My friends chimed in one after another:

"Taking a year off was the best thing I ever did."

"You won't regret it."

❧ ❧ ❧

The Personnel Committee voted in favor of me returning for another year as their pastor. I told the Personnel Committee I wouldn't be able to give them my response until next month.

I sputtered, "People are upset with me all the time."

One member said, "Teresa, you are a breath of fresh air. Of course it ruffles feathers."

I fussed with God, *What do you want me to do? What if I took the summer off and then went back to serve the church in the fall? They want me to come back. I am not a quitter.*

I prayed harder.

Driving through town on the way to the hospital the sign hit me, *Let go of the net.* I saw it with my spiritual eyes and recognized this was God speaking to me to have faith and follow into the unknown. But still I cried out, *You called me into this. You formed me to be a pastor.*

God answered, "I am calling you out to rest."

I announced my decision and stopped swimming against the tide. I floated on my back, steadied by God.

SLAYING THE MONSTER

- What conflict did Teresa encounter? What did she do? Why?
- List the many ways of handling conflict, and the results you have seen.
- Share how you have resolved conflict in your own life.
- How have you heard the voice of God?

- Have you shared your raw emotions with God?
- Find a lament psalm that echoes a situation in your life or the world.

MORE: LAMENT PSALMS INFORMATION

The Psalms of Lament are a guide for us when we suffer. They show us what to do. Take our troubles and share them with God and other people of faith, that they might pray for us and support us.

There is a Pattern in the lament psalms, according to Walter Brueggemann. They move from *Orientation* to *Disorientation* to *New Orientation*.

The Psalms Show Us that God welcomes us when we share our gut reactions, raw emotions. God wants to know what we think and how we feel. These psalms prove that you won't be struck down by lightning if you question God.

If God Knows Everything, Why Do I Need to Tell God Anything? God already knows. It's like this: You have a precious lamp in your home. One other person is home with you. You leave the house. When you come home the lamp is broken.

Do you want the person to a) lie to you, b) say nothing, or c) tell the truth? Most people agree they want to hear the truth. But if you already know they broke the lamp why do you want them to tell you about it?

Communication builds relationships. Silence creates distance and isolation. The road to healing is through communication with God and others. The lament Psalms were written so that the suffering of an individual or community would be lifted up in worship. We are called to stand with those who suffer.

Assurance: Lament Psalms include: 3, 4, 5, 7, 9–10, 13, 14, 17, 22, 25, 26, 27, 28, 31, 36, 39, 40:12–17, 41, 42–43, 52, 53, 54, 55, 56, 57, 59, 61, 64, 70, 71, 77, 86, 89, 120, 139, 141, 142, 12, 44, 58, 60, 74, 79, 80, 83, 85, 89, 90, 94, 123, 126, 129.

Making Sense of Suffering: Lament for a Son by Nicholas Wolterstroff offers a quick read that discusses our deepest questions when we are suffering.

18

Climbing Out of the Pit

IT WAS DECIDED. My girl and I would go to the Grand Canyon! Yee Haw. Away we went. The book of Mark, chapter six, popped up on religious radio stations across the South.

"Jesus said, *Come away to a deserted place all by yourselves and rest awhile.*"

Apparently God didn't want me to forget why I was taking the year off. We stopped to attend church one Sunday. The sermon was based on Psalm forty-six, verse ten.

"*Be still and know that I am God!*" We drank in visits to friends' homes, sat in mourning with friends in Mississippi, climbed up the white sand dunes of New Mexico, and slid into Arizona in time to celebrate a friend's graduation. The trip restored my sense of being wanted and loved just as I was.

On the way home to Virginia I stopped in Chicago to attend the International Clergywomen's Consultation. While there I led workshops on Unseen Footprints: Discovering a Theology of Suffering. The number of registrants overwhelmed the space available.

My soul was being restored, bit by bit, and the call was clear. Write a book. Write your life story. Make it clear so others will know there is hope and healing. So I began to write.

A few months later, I drove to the mountains to lead a retreat. The Blue Ridge Mountains swept me along south to Camp Overlook. The lodge was a welcome place after spending the last half hour wound up over whether I could find the place in the growing dark. The director had left me a welcoming note. I was glad to be alone in the cavernous lodge. Lugging in books and bags, communion elements and juice, I chose a room and sank in.

After a short rest, I prayed, *Dear Lord, May what I say and do be pleasing in your sight.* I fasted while drinking juice, setting up the book table, and working to create a sign saying, "Lay all your burdens down" in multi colors. My stomach nudged me and I prayed again, *Thank you Jesus for bringing me to this place, may the words of my mouth and the meditation of our hearts bring healing.*

I prayed as I smoothed the wrinkles out of the altar cloth. *Bring your holiness and fill this room.* I felt the Spirit enter the room like silent snow falling. I was right where God wanted me to be.

When everyone had gathered, I led them in a guided imagery meditation.

"It's helpful if you place your feet flat on the floor," I told the participants. "Close your eyes. Take deep breaths. Belly breaths. As you breathe in, breathe in the Holy Spirit. As you breathe out, exhale everything that weighs on you."

"Settle in. Go to your favorite place; the place you go to relax. Now imagine sitting in your favorite place. Get comfortable." I paused to allow people a chance to settle into their favorite places. "Imagine you are sitting knee to knee with yourself. Look into your eyes, what do you see? What is there that you should know?" I waited for people, giving them time to be present in the moment.

Then I invited them, "Imagine you are sitting knee to knee with Jesus. He is talking to you. He gathers you in, cheek to cheek and whispers to you." I waited until I sensed people beginning to stir. "You see Jesus go. Still you are relaxed and feel the Holy presence of God. Rest in this moment."

I paused for a long moment then said, "As you come back into this space, gradually open your eyes."

A holy silence filled the room. We rested in it. Then we joined in singing, "Turn Your Eyes Upon Jesus." The retreat moved forward, led by God.

∾∾∾

February found me dancing in the kitchen with my girl. She was twisting away. My brain was dancing with the impossibility of the situation. I had managed to create a Web site for my new business New Pathways —Your Spiritual Guide from Suffering to Hope and Healing. Who would believe it?

Before long I was in Carol's office doing my "check-in" for mental health. We hadn't seen each other in weeks. I recounted the events: possible skin cancer on my nose (would know in a week or two); Pap smear "unusual," come back in three months; holding open houses every weekend on Saturday and Sunday in an attempt to sell the house ourselves; and more.

I said I had maxed out a week and a half or two ago with anxiety: negative thoughts, legs jerking in my sleep, so exhausted, taking a daily nap, and more. What should I do?

Carol said, "You could check out *The Anxiety and Phobia Workbook.*" I brought the book home and checked out the section on over-thinking. I felt disgusted—I already knew this stuff.

It was time to mow the lawn. I climbed on the riding mower and had a conversation with God.

God, you know I don't want to move. What do you want from me?

God said, *Willingness. I want you to be willing.*

I responded by wailing, *Noooooooooo. Ahhhhhhhh.*

But I tried on willingness and it helped. The book suggested visualization and word responses to over-thinking. So I chose the response "React or Response." When the "I wish I were dead" thoughts arrived in my head, I would envision a gun at my head. The gun was the kind where you pull the trigger and a sign saying, "Bang" pops out of it instead of a bullet. Then I would see the gun fall down. It helped that it was a silly response.

Next I asked God, *If I have to be willing, and I have to do these hard things, can't I at least have the peace that passes all understanding?*

God said, *It's yours anytime you want it. All you have to do is be open to it.*

My reaction, *Humph.*

Each night when I went to bed I imagined literally opening my chest where the sternum was. While I did deep breathing, I imagined God pouring peace into my chest. There was so much peace it flowed everywhere! Down my neck, over the top of my head, around my heels, and between my toes went the peace. It flowed back up to my heart covering my back and arms on the way. I felt God's Spirit flowing over and through me with peace.

I told Carol of my major triumph, "I went in to see the dermatologist; the nurse took my blood pressure. I decided to do deep breathing while she took my blood pressure. Two deep breaths and it was over. Result: 110/60."

"What else is new?" Carol asked.

"I'm really struggling with Jesus suffering and God allowing Jesus to suffer."

Carol said, "Why don't you journal to Jesus about it?"

I protested, "Not Jesus. Jesus makes me angry—all this crucifixion, suffering stuff. I don't want to connect with him. So I keep journaling to God."

Driving home I was relieved to not feel all emptied out or stirred up like I did sometimes. I felt fairly peaceful and triumphant. I decided I would journal to Jesus exactly what I thought. When I went to do it I realized I didn't really know what I thought but I did know I was angry.

In May, Ted and I went out to dinner for our anniversary that same night. He gave me a poignant card, a bracelet, and earrings.

Laughingly he said, "Our girl hopes you won't like these or that they won't fit so she can have them." I liked them very much and put on the bracelet right away.

In August, we were still unpacking boxes; although we'd moved in June. The gift of kayaking, made possible by a friend who loaned us the kayaks, helped restore my soul.

Preaching here and there reminded me that the need for hope was large and immediate. Going back and forth to the federal penitentiary, and being with the inmates on their faith journeys through Kairos International, pushed me to stay close to God.

∽∽∽

The road stretched out in front of me, as I drove back to Virginia following a trip to visit my parents and siblings. I'd made a new vow. I was going to try and balance the bad memories with some of the good memories. Were there good memories? Yes. But I'd not focused on them. They didn't have the same power as the ones of terror and rage. Our brains are designed to capture trauma and remember it. Trauma actually shapes the formation of our brain when we are children.

Was my dad different now? Yes. Age had mellowed him. No. He didn't seem to be any better equipped to deal with the ups and downs of life. Did I love him? Absolutely. What about my family as a whole? I feel supported by them and love each of them with my whole heart. I am glad they are my family.

My new counselor, Laura was trained in cognitive therapy.

She asked me, "Is everything the same as it was twenty years ago?" I was brought up short by the question.

"No, things are not the same. I am head and shoulders above where I was twenty years ago." There in my mind spun the words: hope, healing, future, and blessing.

God continues to speak to me. God tells me to, "Go and share the hope, speak of the healing, witness to the blessing."

SLAYING THE MONSTER

- I do it over and over again. I become aware of something that doesn't belong in my life. I see it. What do you see that doesn't belong?

- Then I head off to learn more. What new thing are you aware of and learning more about?

- When I learn the new thing and act on it, I work hard to celebrate my action. I celebrate silly things like when I complete a Sudoku. I give myself a smiley face and an "A+." I do it to continually work on understanding how much I am worth in the eyes of God. Self-esteem is a life-long lesson for me. What about you? What are you acting upon?

- How are you celebrating your journey towards wholeness, healing and the Holy?

MORE: ALL THINGS WORK TOGETHER

Assurance: My life is a testament to the way all things work for good for those who love the Lord. Sometimes I wish that there was no such thing as suffering. What makes all the difference for me is that when I suffer, I know God can and will use it if I am willing to share it with others (Romans 8:28).

What does that mean for me now? I understand that depression and dysthymia are a part of my life. I continue to take medication, and receive counseling in one form or another, and work towards slaying the monster's impact on my life.

Even though the precancerous condition is gone from my nose, I now have an autoimmune condition. The book of Romans, chapter eight, pushes me to pray, *Thank you God for whatever is happening to me. I know it will be used for your glory.* It's not an easy prayer, but I believe it's the right one.

I continue to follow God's guidance ministering through New Pathways, guiding people spiritually from suffering to hope and healing. The website is: www.newpathways.us.

What about Jesus? A year later, I'm still journaling to Jesus and we are getting to know each other in new ways. I still wrestle with Jesus about suffering, but at least we're talking. There is healing in that.